FISHFRIARS HALL REVISITED

WORLD

CONFECTUS FLASHA BRITANNICUS

"Take the Sweets and Think of England"

FISHFRIARS HALL REVISITED

THE DIARY OF A SPOTTY YOUNG ERK

CHRIS TARRANT
AND
TONY NICHOLSON

A STAR BOOK

Published by
the Paperback Division of
W.H. ALLEN & Co. PLC.

A Star Book
Published in 1985
by the Paperback Division of
WH Allen & Co PLC
44 Hill Street, London W1X 8LB

First published in Great Britain

Printed in Great Britain by
Anchor Brendon Ltd, Tiptree, Essex

ISBN 0 352 31768 X

Thanks to Nicki Cohen, Philippa Hargreaves
and Jeremy Loyd

Photographs by Dennis Akerman

FISHFRIARS HALL REVISITED is broadcast on the
Chris Tarrant show on Capital Radio

Designed by Michael Brett

HERE IT IS! AT LAST!

The book that everyone's been talking about . . . Mary Whitehouse . . . The Vice Squad . . . the publishers' lawyers . . .

It started as a dream, and many people say it should have stayed as one . . . but no! It's turned into a fully-fledged nightmare.

It's about as welcome as a pint of creme de menthe, a turkey sandwich and twelve Lords-a-leaping on the twelfth day of Christmas.

It's the public school yarn with the plot that races along like a slug on vallium.

It's . . .

FISHFRIARS HALL REVISITED

AUTHOR'S PREFACE

Fishfriars Hall Revisited follows a long tradition of fish-frying dramas of public school life, like … *Goodbye Mr Chips* … and R. F. Delderfield's classic, *To Serve Them All Fried Plaice* … and is stolen outrageously from *Billy Bunter Turns Cannibal And Eats The Entire Under-Fifteen Rugby Team.*

We have to admit that some of our screenplays have failed, due only to unfortunate timing. *The Tesco Chainstore Massacre* is a perfect example … and our vegetarian movie, *Lentil,* which was to have featured Soya Wilcox and Marlon Branbud … but with this book we firmly believe we have plumbed previously unfathomed depths of inconsequence.

Fishfriars Hall Revisited has a plot which rips along like a freshly kneecapped tortoise, and reveals more of the hidden truth of life in an exclusive boys' public school than 'Bullseye.'

We feel, however, that we should warn readers that this book enters the realms of 'Hard Corn' and, as such, it is unsuitable for children – come to think of it, it's not really suitable for adults either.

Finally, as you read the following chapters, bear in mind the immortal words of Mrs Abraham Lincoln: 'You deserve shooting for bringing me to this rotten play...'

WHAT THE CRITICS SAY ABOUT

FISHFRIARS HALL REVISITED

The Guardian –
''Hilarious' isn't the word! ... Neither is 'clever', 'enjoyable,' or 'good'.'

The Psychic News –
'The sequel will be better.'

The Angling Times –
'It's alright, but there isn't enough fishing in it.'

Film 85 –
'If *Alien* tore you apart ... if *The Texas Chainsaw Massacre* cut you up ... if you were choked by *The Boston Strangler*, then *Fishfriars Hall* will certainly teach you a lesson.'

The Sun –
'*Fishfriars Hall* makes *Crossroads* seem trivial.'

Titbits –
'*Fishfriars Hall* is more gripping than watching your smalls go round at the launderette ... more terrifying than feeding the goldfish ... more fun than finding a slug in your ham salad ... but only just.'

RSPCA Bulletin –
'Full of satire with marginally less bite than a hamster with its teeth kicked in.'

Sue Ellen Fan Club Newsletter –
'The jokes in this book are so old and feeble, they make Joan Collins look positively sprightly.'

Film-Makers Weekly –
'... so played out and stuck for ideas that even the director of *Rocky IV* sneered at it.'

Melody Maker –
'This book has marginally less to say for itself than Prince.'

AND WHAT DO THE STARS HAVE TO SAY

ALEXEI SAYLE –

'I was offended by the bad taste.'

BERNARD MANNING –

'Too smutty! I was shocked!'

JIMMY CRICKET–

'Too silly!'

BENNY HILL–

'Not subtle enough!'

THE KRANKIES–

'We found the photographs of an adult dressed up as a schoolboy nauseating!'

MARY WHITEHOUSE–

'It's the most depraved book I've ever been subjected to – I had to read it three or four times just be to sure.'

THE POPE–

'It's a belter!'

Me having a light snack
(din-dins was inedible)

TUESDAY SEPTEMBER 3RD

Dear Diary

Today was my first day at Fishfriars Hall, a school famous for its discipline, academic achievement, and sordid exposés in *The News Of The World*...

The great academy prides itself in taking mere children and painstakingly transforming them into chinless, tweedy twerps with a penchant for killing foxes. Even under-achievers at Fishfriars usually go on to get some sort of job, however menial, like — Cabinet Ministers with names like Geoffrey and Norman...

The school had to move with the times and adopt new traditions from the State Comprehensives, like — burning down classrooms and welly-sniffing...

My father, who had been to Fishfriars thirty years before me, said he owed everything to the harsh, spartan lifestyle and the frequent beatings — his constant twitch; his bed wetting; and his love of walking round the house in mater's undies. I had to admit dear diary that I was secretly pleased that the school had gone what dear papa called 'namby-pamby', by abolishing hanging... Although I was soon to learn to my cost that the Headmaster had retained the use of 'The Cat' for severe punishments — he used to tease it and pull its tail until it was really cross, and then put it down your trousers...

TUESDAY SEPTEMBER 3RD

My heart was pounding as we approached the famous school gates. 'Whoa! Stop outside the gates Walter!' called my dear papa. Walter's trusty old brakes gripped just in time and we stopped. 'Why do you call your bicycle Walter?' I asked my dearest daddy. 'Because it's a Raleigh son!' he replied whimsically. . . well, not very whimsically. . . well, hardly whimsically at all actually. He prised me out of the basket on the handlebars with a couple of tyre levers and then leaned forward and put his head on my shoulders. . . but it looked ridiculous on my little body, so he put it back on his own.

'There you are son,' said the dear man, 'a tuck parcel from dear mater and myself.' I must admit I was a little disappointed at the contents, but I didn't dare show it in front of dear, kind papa. . . 'Oh lovely father!' I said, 'Turnips!'

'Aye lad' he said enviously, 'Turnips!. . . If only I was young again!'

He asked me how I was fixed for spending-money, so I gave him a fiver to be going on with. On parting he gave me one final piece of advice. . . 'Don't forget son — always wear your boxing gloves in bed. . . and never get in a lift with anyone on the "F-Plan" diet. . .'

These final words brought a lump to my throat and tears to my eyes — he'd been gripping me by the windpipe! I bade him a tearful farewell, and it was with a heavy heart that I struggled up the great gravel drive with my suitcase, my boxing-gloves and my turnips.

I wondered how long it would be before I would be subjected to the customary harmless pranks that chaps play on new boys. At that moment rough hands grabbed me and nailed me to a tree. I was then de-bagged and my underpants were filled with 'Fiery Jack' and sulphuric acid. This, along with relentless blows to my solar plexus made me lose consciousness. How they laughed! I later learned that the staff do this to all new boys.

You'll never know the joy, dear diary, that I felt as I caught sight of three smiling pupils who came running up to share my burden. With cheery 'Hallos' they picked up my heavy things and skipped off down the winding drive towards the great Hall. . . I never saw them — or my luggage — ever again!

As I ate my first lunch at Fishfriars Hall I began to fully appreciate the meaning of the word 'diabolical'.

Ten minutes later I was leaving the canteen at some speed — when I quite literally bumped into Matron, sending her sprawling across the floor. As she picked herself up, the first thing that struck me was her unusual crocodile-skin handbag. . . the second thing that struck me was her clenched fist. She was not what I had expected at all — beautifully-coiffeured dark hair. . . on the backs of her hands; a candy-striped pinafore dress with a somewhat daring slit. . . right across her bosom; fish-net tights. . . you could tell they were fish-nets because they had big cork floats at six-inch intervals. Realising I was a new boy she swallowed her anger. Unfortunately she also swallowed her bubbly-gum and coughed her head off. Eventually we got her head back on again and she tucked me under one muscular arm and carried me to the Sick Bay.

She informed me that all new boys had to have a Medical and she was the only Medical in the school, if I got her drift. I didn't. She then told me she was going to slip into something cooler and, sure enough, she promptly skidded across the floor and into a tin bath full of ice cream. Matron huskily offered to let me eat the ice cream off her, but I declined as I hadn't got a spoon on me. She seemed to be getting a bit cross for some reason — like Mummy gets when she catches Pater wearing her undies. Quickly Matron tore all her clothes off and told me I could have anything I wanted. 'That's very kind' I said, 'I'll have your brassiere — it'll make a super catapult. . .'

She irritably asked me how old I was. I told her I was twenty-eight, but that I'd had trouble graduating in elementary plasticine-snake-rolling and didn't leave Playschool until I was nineteen. She called me a 'silver-tongued cream-horn', grabbed me by the ears and pulled my head into her chest. . .

'I think the bell's gone Matron,' I pleaded.

She just agreed and said that the thieving swine at Fishfriars Hall would swipe anything. Her breathing was quickening, she called me a naughty boy and said she was afraid she was weakening. As I failed to respond, basically because I didn't know what she was talking about — she let go and decided to medically examine me. She took my temperature, my pulse and my gold wrist-watch. . . then I had to cross my legs while she took a mallet from her desk drawer. She hit me hard between the eyes. I screamed. 'Reflexes normal,' she wrote down.

She then put her ear to my mouth and asked me to

put out my tongue. 'Ooh, that's lovely!' she said, her eyes glazing over. I was then asked to read the card on the wall: 'Dear Matron, Having a lovely time hiking in The Lake District. I'm writing this in my sleeping-bag. Wish you were here. Love, Dangler Major, School Rugby Captain.' Apparently Matron and Dangler Major had attempted the Pennine Way together during half-term hols — because they were sick of the usual way and the French Way's bad for your back.

Matron then leapt to her feet, grabbed me firmly by the instrument trolleys and made me cough. This she did by puffing the acrid smoke from her pipe into my face.

At length she declared me A1 for physical fitness and Z-minus for masculinity. Before I took my leave I asked if she would come and take a look at Sidney, my pet hamster, which was rather ill. . . in fact I thought it had got Gerbil Measles. I made him a little sick-bed out of a pocket handkerchief strung up between two posts in our dormitory. She refused point-blank to come with me but, after much persuasion, she grudgingly agreed to have a look at him if I brought him to her office. . . which just goes to prove that. . . 'If the Matron won't come to my hammock, then my hammock must go to the Matron. . .'

As I lie in my steaming pit this first night at Fishfriars I muse on whether mater has packed me off with last year's cricket trousers — now three sizes too small — and would it have an adverse effect on my googlies! And how come Matron wouldn't come out to a case of Gerbil Measles when everyone knows she drops everything for a case of cheap Champagne.

My new chum Cowardly Major arriving at the start of a new term

THURSDAY SEPTEMBER 19TH

Dere Dowry

I must say I am settling down nicely at Fishfriars, and thoroughly enjoying life in my particular house. The school houses are all named after previous headmasters. For instance, the extremely musical headmaster, Professor Minim, has a house named after him — 'Minim House'; all the really naughty boys were despatched to Dogg House; but me and my chums were moved to the most modern pre-fab dorm, which was unfortunately plagued by rising damp, dry rot and subsiding foundations — Yes! We are in Council House. Strangely, Fishfriars Hall chose to ignore its last headmaster, Dr Brick-Shippe, when it was naming its houses. . .

All us chaps in Council House had a lively discussion about who was having which bunk. During this discussion I lost four teeth and a couple of pints of blood. Cowardly Major, our dormitory bully, gave Wimp Minor a Chinese Burn — he shoved his head in a pan of boiling Chop Suey. . . then, on merely being debagged and threatened with an electric cattle-prod, the young wimp graciously agreed to sleep standing on his head in the lavatory. Methane Minor, the ever-flatulent fifth former, was placed on the top bunk by the window, with an early-warning wind-sock tied to the bottom of his bed.

At that moment in walked the Headmaster who said we were to have a new, somewhat anti-social inmate by the name of Peabody. . . 'Oh no! Not Sprinkler Peabody the school bed-wetter!' We all groaned. 'The very same!' smirked the Arch-Beako putting on his waterproof overshoes before going to get the young chap in question. Cowardly Major organised a bit of a reshuffle to house Sprinkler Peabody. He was given a top bunk — above Wimp Minor. Wimp Minor, not daring to argue, went to find his umbrella. . .

Squinter Binns, the school pervert, despatched himself, his torch and his pile of dirty books to a dark and dingy corner and lay there demonstrating great manual dexterity and proving that Matron's efforts to curtail his night manoeuvres had failed, by peeling an orange while wearing his boxing-gloves.

It was getting close to 'lights-out' and Sprinkler Peabody decided to have a drink of water — in fact he drank the entire contents of a five-gallon fire bucket, and was making a start on the goldfish tank. Poor little Wimp Minor burst into tears and went to find his sou'wester and wellies as well.

We all needed to let off steam before bed-time and, after a hearty supper of sprouts, lentils and a glass of boiling water, that's exactly what Methane Minor did.

Suddenly there was a 'whoop' of delight from Sprinkler Peabody — he had found a crate of cold lager and was drinking one bottle after another. Poor little Wimp Minor, in the bunk below, begged for mercy and started building an 'Ark'. . .

Fagging was an established tradition in Council House, but our senior boy — Capitalist-Swine Major —

was trying to give up 'fags'. . . That is, ever since a fellow-prefect, Twitte Major, had asked his fag, Frankie Bruno, a perfectly reasonable favour — to lick his bedroom floor clean — and young Bruno had gone berserk, shouting, 'Do you think I'm going simple??! Do you think that Frankie has gone to wally-hood??' And with that he pulled Twitte Major's head through his own letter-box. This finally convinced Capitalist-Swine Major that fags can seriously damage your health.

Meanwhile, Cowardly Major, our dormitory bully, was busy organising a series of sadistic initiation ceremonies for potential fags. He cleverly devised each one to suit the various first formers' names: Dock-Leaffe Junior was thrown into the school nettles, and poor old Christian Minor was thrown to the school lions; young Tristram Blacke and Decker Minor were kneecapped with an electric drill attachment; Winterbottom had his underpants filled with snow and ice; Andover was tied up with his *'and over* a candle flame for 10 minutes — and young Bolsover did a runner and was never seen again!

It was school tradition that this cruelty was to be borne without any flinching, cringing or wincing — but this was surely impossible for poor old Biggins Minor, who was strapped in a chair and forced to watch endless re-runs of 'Surprise, Surprise' — God how he suffered.

The last was a young Canadian lad called Wholemeal. Cowardly Major decided to bake him in the oven like a gingerbread man. Wisely, Wholemeal slipped on a pair of jodhpurs and a big hat before going into the oven and came out as a Canadian gingerbread policeman! He then took Cowardly Major off for routine questioning — knowing just where to hit him so that it wouldn't leave any marks. The moral of this tortuous tale, dear hanging-on-for-grim-death diary, is. . . 'Don't bake a Mounty out of a Wholemeal'. . .

As I lie tonight in my steaming sack, I ponder on this teaser. . . Will young Wholemeal be the subject of next week's 'This is Your Loaf'?

CONFECTUS FLASHA
BRITANNICUS
"Take the Sweets and Think of England"
FISHFRIARS
HALL
SCHOOL
PROSPECTUS

SCHOOL MOTTO-
"CONFECTUS FLASHA BRITANNICUS"

A WORD ABOUT OUR PRINCIPAL

Quintin Carruthers Frotter, Doctor (Struck-off)
Headmaster Fishfriars Hall and Proprietor of Fishfriars Hall Ltd — suppliers of First Class Pigswill, schoolboys and Latex Leisure-wear to the gentry.

Age — Indeterminate
Current Contract — Indefinite
Marital Status — In jeopardy
Cheques — In the post 
Background — Educated here at Fishfriars Hall, where he held the position of School Dunce for six years. Failed every exam, medical and aptitude test, was about to be publicly humiliated and expelled for inordinate stupidity when he inherited a large sum of money in a Swiss Bank Account and was immediately made Headboy with special privileges (first crack at Matron, smaller portions of canteen food, etc.). Careers Officer couldn't think of a proper job he was capable of doing, so he became a teacher. Swiss Bank Account still holding out, he was offered a job at Fishfriars Hall. It was soon discovered that he couldn't teach either, so he seemed ideally suited for the post of Headmaster. It is ironic that he was appointed as a natural to practice as Headmaster, and yet has turned out to enjoy some of the most unnatural practices of any other Headmaster in the history of Fishfriars Hall. Was given an Honorary Doctorate by the University of Kuala Lumpor for services to the rubber industry, but was 'struck-off' shortly afterwards when they found out what he was doing with said rubber. Sent down for a long stretch.

Quintin Carruthers Frotter

Dr Frotter is a very active member of the local community. He is Parliamentary Candidate for the "Come-Back-Atilla-The-Hun-All-Is-Forgiven Party," and is an ardent supporter of the reintroduction of Capital Punishment (in schools). He is also a J.P. and sits on the local bench... near the duck-pond, where he offers local boy scouts sweets and encourages them to try on thigh-length waders filled with custard. He is also in favour of bringing back the cat (some say fingers down the throat should do the trick, others say it serves him right for eating the school curry in the first place). For appearances sake he married the daughter of Lord Ballcock, the chamberpot and bidet tycoon... Yes dear about-to-be-taken-for-a-ride parent, it was a marriage of convenience.

THE SCHOOL

Fishfriars Hall set itself up against other more famous Public Schools and had to start from the very bottom. It has always been well suited there. The school is progressive in terms of discipline. The Headmaster has progressed from the cane to the 3-tailed horse-whip.

Fishfriars Hall prides itself in being one of the first boys' Public Schools to introduce girls into the Sixth Form. We are proud to say that we have been successful in turning them into fine educated women and fit mothers for the next generation — many of them whilst still at the school.

A WORD OF ADVICE FOR NEW BOYS

Think twice before resisting unnatural sexual advances — it may well be a future Tory Cabinet Minister.

SCHOOL FEES

Negotiable. Mr Don Corleoni, the Italian Master, and some of his boys will call round. (Message from Mr Don Corleoni — "You are requested to pay promptly — accidents can happen and, whilst we all hope your boys will end up pillars of the community, you probably don't want them to end up pillars of the proposed new fly-over — if you get my meaning...").

The last headmaster of Fishfriars Hall, Dr. Strangeways, seen here shortly before his arrest.

SATURDAY OCTOBER 5TH

Back Again Dear Diary

It is the end of my first month at Fishfriars Hall. Things can only get better. I slept like a log the other night — they had locked me in the Wood Shed, just for putting a ferret down Wimp Minor's Y-fronts and super-gluing them top and bottom. My house prefect caught me and he gave me six strokes on the seat of my trousers. . . then he started stroking the back of my neck, so I beat a hasty retreat before things got out of hand.

Being locked in the Wood Shed was horrible. On the floor was a severed hand and a little axe covered in blood. . . I'd heard about Matron's drastic remedies for nose-pickers and nail-biters. The various cutting tools had a curiously morbid attraction. I attempted to get the huge saw with the wicked-looking blade of cold steel out of temptation's way by rubbing it with Vaseline — I'd heard that Vaseline gets rid of cold saws. . . But the massive axe which leaned against the wall kept haunting me with the urge to chop my own foot off. . . It would get me free admission to the local 'Hop'. . . and think of the saving on socks! It would only be a temporary measure of course, because Mummy had said I would grow another foot before I left school, and I didn't need three.

The door of the Wood Shed opened at supper-time

and I hungrily ate what the duty prefect threw in. . . which was unfortunate as it turned out to be a pillow and a blanket, which gave me awful indigestion! As they let me out in the morning I blinked in the bright sunlight, but I smiled a self-contented smile at my fortitude and self-control. . . I had undergone the entire Wood Shed episode, dear Diary, without using a single joke about choppers, big or otherwise. Back in the school entrance hall I hurriedly counted my feet to check that the urge to chop one off hadn't got the better of me in the middle of the night. I don't know what I should have done if it had — I would have been stumped! There was no hair growing on the palms of my hands either, so presumably I had slept well.

I suddenly got the feeling I wasn't alone — I could tell because I was receiving repeated blows with a gravel-filled handbag. I looked up and saw Matron in a high dudgeon. . . and a low blouse.

She wanted me to meet her in the potting sheds at midnight, for a game of 'Mummys and Daddys'. 'Oh, I know,' I said enthusiastically, 'I go out, get drunk and throw up on the cat, and you hide behind the door without your teeth in and hit me over the head with the coal shovel. . .'

Matron knitted her brow. . . and made it into a lovely Fair-Isle sweater. . . then she gave me a head butt, lit up her pipe and disappeared.

Feeling confused and rather homesick, I made my way to the school chapel, or The Sanctuary, as it was known. Nervously I knocked on the imposing chapel door. The school chaplain opened the door irritably and glared at me.

SATURDAY OCTOBER 5TH

'Good morning Chaplain — or may I call you Charlie?' I said whimsically. I was rewarded for my humorous jest with a crack on the head with a huge leather-bound Bible. I noticed that the Chaplain was busy inflating a blow-up rubber Joan of Arc, presumably as a Chapel decoration. Nevertheless I asked him if he could spare me a few minutes.

'Sod off, zit-face!' he snapped, 'I only work Sundays!' Then, because I wouldn't go away, he asked me how I could believe in a God that had given me ears like hub-caps and a face like a baboon's bum.

I wondered if he was in the right job. Eventually he let me into The Sanctuary and asked me another profound theological question:

'Why did God create man in his own perfect image on the sixth day, rest on the seventh and then spend the eighth creating B.O. and piles?' I didn't have a ready answer, so I asked him a question. I asked him why he wore a dress, to which he replied that it was in fact a habit, and I said, 'Yes, and a very strange habit too, if I may say so.' This brought forth another clout on the head with the Bible.

Then we prayed together. He prayed for his rich Aunt Gladys to drop dead and I prayed to get out alive. He then showed me his pet snail that he said he kept to symbolise the Church's policy on moving with the times. He kept it in a place of honour in The Sanctuary.

I felt we were forming some sort of rapport so I started to confess my sins to him. He stared at me oddly and lit a fat cigarette. It smelled ever so funny — I think it must have been incense. Suddenly he started to giggle and speak in tongues. His eyes glazed over as he inhaled the incense and he rolled about on the floor singing a strange hymn to a little known Eskimo saint named Nell. He was obviously casting out a demon. As he writhed around I averted my eyes as he was wearing no knickers underneath his habit. I tactfully left him, a little disappointed at the guidance he had given me but satisfied in the knowledge that I was one of the few pupils that could honestly say, Dear Dumbfounded Diary, that they'd seen the knickerless parson's snail of The Sanctuary. . .

At the end of the day as I lie ruminating in my putrefying pit I find myself pondering: If ten cubic inches of feathers weighs the same as eight grams of sawdust, how long would it take the average farmyard hen to lay a suite of furniture. . .??

MONDAY OCTOBER 28TH

Dire Diary

I woke up to what seemed a perfectly normal day at Fishfriars Hall. Cowardly Major, the dormitory bully, had garotted a couple of youngsters as they slept. . . Sparky Butane, the school arsonist's bed was on fire. . . Squinter Binns was exploring under his bed-clothes with a torch. . . Methane Minor's blankets were billowing and hovering six inches above his bed. . . and poor old Limp Minor, who sleeps above him, was unconscious as usual.

'Ouch! Crikey and bother!' I said — or Anglo-Saxon words to that effect — as I smashed my toe against something very hard. Someone had given me a plum-pie bed — it was a bit like an apple-pie bed, but it had big stones in it.

'Come on out Big Stones!' I yelled. Big Stones clambered out looking rather sheepish — he has a white curly fleece and chews grass.

I got out of bed and took my football boots off — our Headmaster made us wear them in bed to stop us playing soccer with ourselves.

It was, like I said, a perfectly normal day at Fishfriars Hall — that is until morning prayers in the main hall. Dr Frotter, the Headmaster, was smartly dressed in his neatly pressed voluminous black gown — nothing unusual about that you might say, but this

Could I get your Highness another brandy…
or a rampant page 3 girl perhaps?

was a ballroom gown with a full chiffon underskirt and 2½ million sequins hand-sewn on by his mother especially for the occasion. The rest of the staff were all wearing the insignia of their respective qualifications and honours — I could see six cycle proficiency badges, two bronze swimming medals and a Tufty Club sticker from where I was standing. Public schools certainly attract a very special breed of teachers.

'Silence!' bawled Dr Frotter. 'I have something to say that may shock you all! Knickers!!'. He was right, I was shocked! He went on:

'Yesterday morning I caught McCartney Minor carrying a hundredweight of marijuana in his satchel, which I naturally confiscated. Now, therefore, I am compelled to carry out a public flogging!'

'I'll give you two thousand quid for it!' yelled a voice from the back of the hall.

'Done!' said the Headmaster, 'And let that be a warning to you all. Any drugs I confiscate will be publicly flogged the next day!' He then went on to explain why the staff were all dressed up — apparently we were honoured to have a member of the Royal Family joining the school — Prince Luke, or 'Luko' as he preferred to be known, Prince Luko was one of the younger members of the Queen's large family who, due to all the press coverage that the others have had, had been forgotten about by everyone including the Queen and had been discovered at Sandringham after fourteen years playing with bricks and wearing a nappy. Dr Frotter went on to tell us how Prince Luko was to be treated as a perfectly normal pupil and would have no special privileges just because of his royal blood. We were to refer to him simply as 'Your most gracious Royal Highness' and bowing was to be kept to a minimum.

'McGuigan Minor!' The Head yelled, 'You remember how I had to thrash you last week for fighting? Well, if

Prince Luko is caught fighting, the punishment will be exactly the same — I'll give you another thrashing!' At that moment the doors burst open and two of the Prince's personal aides stepped forward — one was all in yellow and the other had a gold ring piercing his left ear — yes, they were a lemon-aide and an earring-aide. . .

Dr Frotter graciously swept down the steps towards the Prince, then he hoovered the Hall floor and polished all the door-knobs.

Prince Luko settled into the school fairly quickly and was treated as a normal pupil — well, except for the fact that the canteen gave him roast swan and larks' tongues in aspic when we were having spam fritters and mushy peas. . . and he didn't have to do any lessons, as an education is considered a drawback to a member of The Royal Family. . . Oh and he was permanently flanked by a group of guards in polished brass armour. Incidentally these guards got into trouble on their first day in the school. Prince Luko had ordered afternoon tea for himself and his entourage, and his guards had got rather out of hand and begun throwing buns and scones at one another. Of course it wasn't long before one had broken a window. The Headmaster naturally made them write out one hundred times, dear bracing-yourself Diary. . . 'People in brass trousers shouldn't throw scones.'

Tonight, as I lie thinking in my pig-sickening put-U-up, I ponder upon the chief bodyguard and personal aide to Prince Luko — would Luko's Aide help him through the day??

FISHFRIARS HALL SCHOOL REPORT

NAME	H.R.H. Prince Luko Windsor		
SUBJECT	ACHIEVEMENT	EFFORT	REMARKS
MATHS	F-	A+	Obviously not his strong subject. (Insists that 4+4 = six fingers and two thumbs.) Nevertheless, what a fine young man!
ENGLISH	F-	A+	Clearly not his best subject. (Thought a 'Subordinate Clause' was one of Father Christmas's junior assistants. Mind you, what a whizzo pupil to teach.
GEOGRAPHY	F-	A+	Not his forte'. (Has an annoying habit of colouring large areas of his atlas red and labelling them 'Mater's!'). I must say though, what a wonderful boy he is.
BIOLOGY ENVIRONMENTAL STUDIES	F-	A+	Following in the true traditions of the rest of his family, he has taken a keen interest in wildlife preservation, and has also joined the local fox hunt and the grouse-shoot. I should add he is my favourite person in the entire universe.
FRENCH			
HISTORY	F-	A+	Not particularly his subject. (Thought 'The Charge of the Light Brigade' was another name for an Electricity Bill) What a Wag though!
SCIENCE			Science is not his particular strength (although he got a distinction in Sex Education) But what a delightful fellow!

TERM MICHAELMAS

SUBJECT	ACHIEVEMENT	EFFORT	REMARKS
ART HANDICRAFTS	A+	A+	A model pupil! (He models for jug handles during pottery classes). A super boy.
GAMES PHYSICAL EDUCATION	F–	A+	NOT HIS THING REALLY. KEEPS FALLING OF HIS HORSE. (HAVE TRIED TO TELL HIM YOU DON'T NEED A HORSE IN CRICKET). HAVING SAID THAT HE IS TRULY A MARVELLOUS CHAP.
RELIGIOUS INSTRUCTION			

GENERAL PROGRESS:
Incredible! He is barely literate, has two left feet and an I.Q that you can count on the thumbs of one hand, and yet he has been offered places at Oxford and Cambridge, he's been accepted as an Admiral in the Navy, a Wing Commander in the RAF; and is on a promise with every girl within a 100 mile radius of Fish-Friars Hall.

ATTENDANCE RARE (but usually sends a servant on his behalf.)

FORM TEACHER'S SIGNATURE Mr Hat-Trick (O.B.E. ??)

HEAD TEACHER'S SIGNATURE Dr Frotter

PARENT'S SIGNATURE HRH MRS E. Windsor

FRIDAY NOVEMBER 8TH

Dead Dribbly

The Headmaster, Dr Frotter, called us all together in the Main Hall today for a special assembly. The preliminaries over with, Wimp Minor was pushed on to the centre of the stage and forced at gun-point to launch into his soprano solo of 'Oh For The Wings Of A Dove', which he did with great gusto — 'The Great Gusto' being the stage name of Methane Minor, the ever-flatulent fifth former, who represented the wind section and accompanied Wimp Minor's vocals with a curiously resonant bass line.

The acne-riddled, Valderma-soaked weed was in full swing, trilling away on the high C's, when suddenly a loud twang was heard, his knees buckled, and his voice cracked discordantly and yodelled tunelessly down a full two octaves. Poor old Wimp Minor was immediately dragged from the hall and flogged mercilessly for reaching puberty without a note of consent from his parents.

The Head then gave a friendly reminder to a list of boys whose parents hadn't yet paid the school fees. He suggested that they inform their fathers that they would receive one of their offsprings' fingers through the post every day until he received their cheques.

Dr Frotter went on to tell us the latest news of Fishfriars Hall. Old Ben Flasher, the school caretaker, had been caught at the weekend by a stroppy policewoman, lingering in the doorway of a canvas marquee at the local garden fete, and was arrested for 'loitering within tent'. It seems his trousers came down last Saturday and his case comes up next Thursday, even though he tried desperately to have it out with the policewoman there and then. The Head mused on who was in the right — was it The Bill, or was it Ben??

The Arch-beako droned on, reading the school notices — 'Keep off the grass'. . . 'Knock before entering'. . . 'No gobbing in the staff-room'. . . and so on. . . until the snoring that echoed round the great hall sounded like a herd of cattle with catarrh. . . Then suddenly, out of the blue, he dropped a real bombshell — In fact it was such a belter that the hall had to be cleared for 10 minutes, with all the doors and windows open. When we all re-assembled he said that he had a notice which would stun us all. . . he then went round the hall hitting us all over the head with it, and he was right — it did! His final announcement was almost as stunning. . . As an experiment in co-education for public schools, a handful of nymphets in gymslips were to be introduced to Fishfriars. A buzz went round the hall. There were screams of pain and panic, and the all-too-familiar crunch of breaking bones — Yes, it was a double-decker buzz!!

Girls in Fishfriars Hall! It seemed about as likely a combination as a third rate geriatric actor in the White House.

Reactions were mixed. Mr Hitler, the Games Master, had a wicked glint in the eye without the monocle and slapped his riding-crop excitedly against

Adjudicators scoring old Ben Flasher in the local 'Indecent Exposure Championship' semi-finals . . .

his jack-booted right leg.

Mr Shirt-Lifter, the Drama Teacher, looked singularly unimpressed by the news. In fact he screwed his face up so much that he smudged his mascara.

Prince Luko, the youngest son of the Royal Family, and next in line for the leading role in Fleet Street's gossip columns, was already sending his footmen out for a case of breath freshener and a crate of powdered rhinos' horn. . . At the thought of the competition our over-sexed Matron's face fell — oddly enough, she looked better without it. . . Within minutes, shares in her Personal Massage Service had dropped to an all-time low.

With all his news delivered, Dr Frotter said as a special treat we were going to have a temperamental Norwegian wine-glass juggler to entertain us — Anna Fiord. . . Unfortunately she was used to playing further North in somewhat colder climates, so she sulked and went home. The moral of this story being, dear long-suffering Diary, 'Never book a miffed Norse in the South.'

And in the wee small hours lying alone in my barbaric-beyond-belief blankets I ponder whether, when our ageing school doctor sees the new girls stripped for a medical, will he have a stroke. . .

CURRICULUM VITAE

Name : Benjamin Seymour Flasher

Current Occupation : School Caretaker, Fishfriars Hall

Age : 63

Marital Status : Available. Genuine offers considered. Ideal partner - rich middle-aged widow, good cook and housekeeper with nubile teenage daughters (Please sent photo of nubile teenage daughters). No cranks please - one in the house is quite enough.

Education : Changed school frequently, due to persistent harassment by a string of girls' mothers. Expelled from school for good at age 14 for failing to wear school uniform for classes - in fact, failing to wear anything for classes. Whilst at school invented a new game - "I'll Show You Mine Whether You Show Me Yours Or Not".

Career :

March 1936 - Apprentice Church Verger. (Asked to leave after being caught with his cassock up round his neck, mooning at the arriving parishioners from the belfry.)

April 1936 - Further Education. (As approved by H.M. Govt.)

June 1941 - Found under stairs in sister's dress eating Call-Up Papers. Volunteered for Army duty upon receiving good kicking from Military Police. During War was never exposed to the 'Front-Line' (but was caught AWOL down the London Underground exposing himself to the District Line). Confined in glasshouse. (Big mistake! - He spent all his time pressed against the glass with his trousers down). Eventually dishonourably discharged amidst much publicity following an unfortunate misunderstanding with the regimental goat.

November 1945 - Freelance mail-bag manufacturer (6 months off

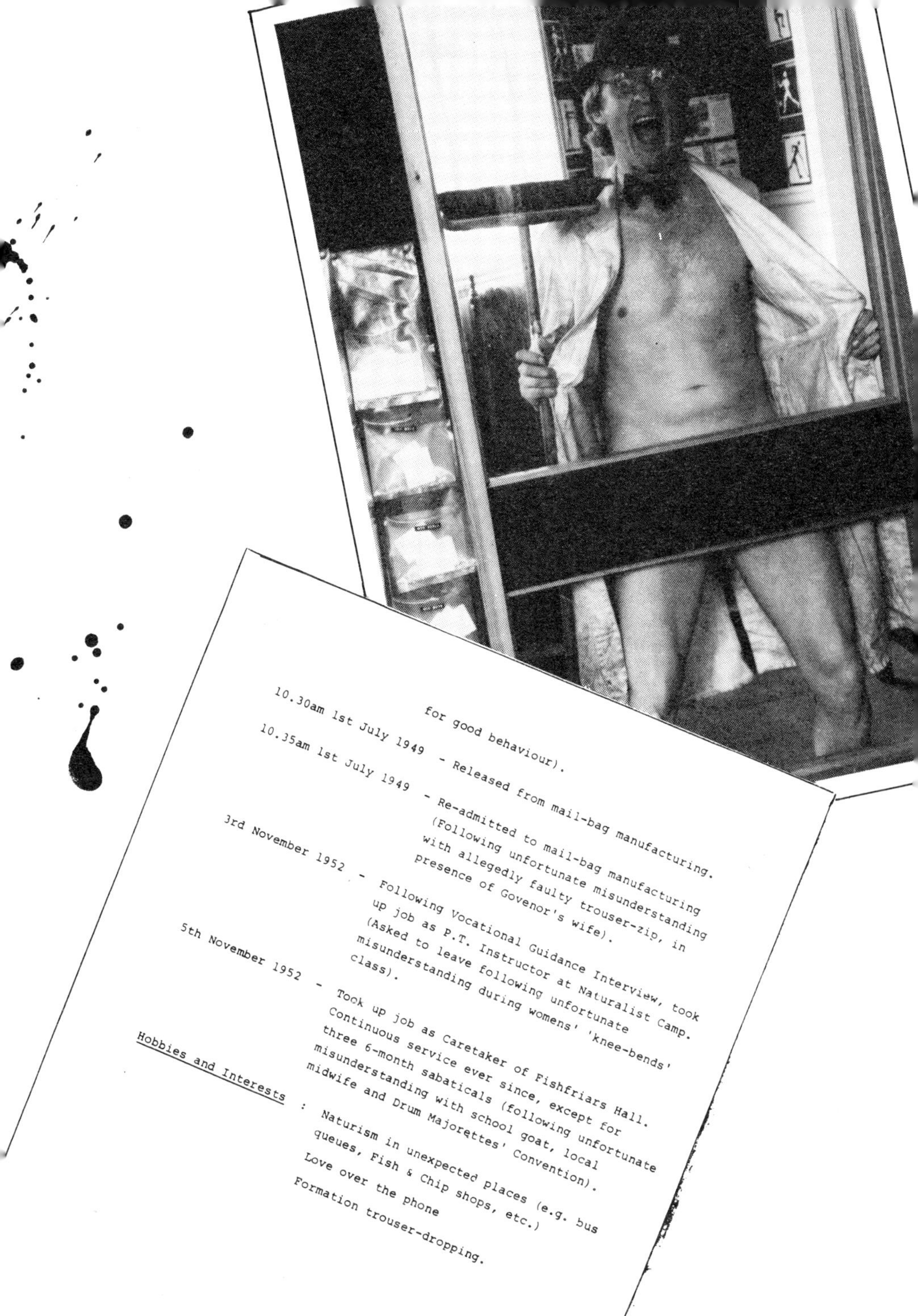

for good behaviour).

10.30am 1st July 1949 - Released from mail-bag manufacturing.

10.35am 1st July 1949 - Re-admitted to mail-bag manufacturing (Following unfortunate misunderstanding with allegedly faulty trouser-zip, in presence of Govenor's wife).

3rd November 1952 - Following Vocational Guidance Interview, took up job as P.T. Instructor at Naturalist Camp. (Asked to leave following unfortunate misunderstanding during womens' 'knee-bends' class).

5th November 1952 - Took up job as Caretaker of Fishfriars Hall. Continuous service ever since, except for three 6-month sabaticals (following unfortunate misunderstanding with school goat, local midwife and Drum Majorettes' Convention).

<u>Hobbies and Interests</u> : Naturism in unexpected places (e.g. bus queues, Fish & Chip shops, etc.)

Love over the phone

Formation trouser-dropping.

FRIDAY DECEMBER 6TH

Beer Brewery

It was 7 o'clock on Friday morning, and I was having trouble getting out of bed — my housemaster kept dragging me back in again. We had to be up early though, because it was Founder's Day at Fishfriars Hall, which meant that our parents were invited to come and spend a totally untypical day in the school, getting completely the wrong impression about normal school-life.

Falsehoods and pretence were the order of the day — the staff were sobered up for 24 hours; the Headmaster, Dr Frotter, pretended to have a sense of humour; and the prefects had all the pin-up photos that they drooled over confiscated, and they were told to put up pictures of girls instead.

The Headmaster gave his usual warnings during assembly about expected behaviour at Founder's Day. McCartney Minor was ordered to keep off the grass! — In fact, he was told to stay out of the way altogether and confine himself to the sunken cellar where they dump the offal for school dinners — in other words, he was given the freedom of the liver-pool. . .

Us chaps had to spend the morning whitewashing the coal and vacuuming the lawn. Wimp Minor volunteered, after losing only three toenails to Cowardly Major's trusty pliers, to clean out the toilet block. A rope was threaded down each loo, and up every U-bend, and was then tied round Wimp Minor's neck. All we had to do was pull on the other end. How we laughed as he disappeared head first down the first bowl, only to reappear a second later, spluttering for air out of the next one. He was carrying a pair of Sweaty Swinton's socks, which we were certain would kill 99% of all known germs, and was instructed to concuss the other 1%, by dropping the nut on them.

The parents arrived at noon. It was an eye-opener to see the chaps' maters and paters. Squinter Binns was dragged out from his dark corner, leaving his torch and his dirty books behind. The poor stunted little wretch blinked blindly in the bright daylight as he greeted his parents. His father's hair had all dropped out, he was wearing two massive hearing-aids and pebble glasses, and he had a hump. His mater, who never said a word, but followed her husband around as if floating on air, had a curiously rubbery appearance and smelt of old wellies.

Cowardly Major, our dormitory bully, met his father's Roll Royce at the gates. Bullying obviously ran in the family — his father was a door-to-door insurance salesman. Mr Cowardly had just re-married and Cowardly Major's step-mother turned out to be a 17-year-old exotic dancer, who was wearing a black leather micro-mini-skirt and fishnet stockings. 'Give your new mummy a kiss,' suggested Mr Cowardly, tweaking his son's ear with a pair of wire-cutters. Ten minutes later buckets of cold water had to be thrown over them before Cowardly Major could be dragged off.

Prince Luko, the youngest member of the Royal

Family, was very excited about his mummy's visit. Dr Frotter, for some strange reason, made a special effort to meet Prince Luko's mum personally. He dragged a bit of red carpet all the way to the bus-stop and then prostrated himself in the gutter.

'My husband and I would like to know how Luko is doing at school', said his mater, whipping off her headscarf and revealing the Imperial Crown. The Head promptly gave Prince Luko another 33 honorary 'A' levels, Captaincy of all the sports teams, a turn at thrashing the first formers, and the special school medal for bravery in war, because he was sure he would earn it if there ever was one. . . Prince Luko's mater was so moved that she told the Head to get on one knee, took out her sword, dubbed him a right crawler and chopped his ears off!. . .

Wimp Minor and his pater, a scrawny little tax collector from Milton Keynes with big ears and bad breath, were holding hands and admiring the roses when Mr Wimp turned, saw Cowardly Major and made an unfortunate comment about the Cowardly family's bandy legs. Cowardly Major forced a polite smile as Mr Wimp patted him patronisingly on the head. Wimp Minor was meanwhile digging himself a grave with his bare hands.

All went well on Founder's Day, until the bloodbath in the Great Hall during the Headmaster's speech. He made a comment about frogs being dissected in biology classes and the Letour family, from the turbulent Basque region of France, took exception, and because they had all been asked to stand in the doorway, no-one was able to get out without getting a good hiding. . . which just goes to show, dear despairing Diary, that you shouldn't put all your Basques in one exit. . .

Tonight as I lie in my heaving hammock, I muse on the Founder's Day girls versus boys rugby match — how did Knee-Trembler Major tackle ten girls and still manage to remain standing??

And was Nureyev Major voted 'Man of the match' for his outstanding tackle??

Prince Luko proving that a little knowledge is a dangerous thing in the hi-tech school laboratory

FISHFRIARS HALL SCHOOL REPORT

NAME	Roger Binns (also known as "Squinter")		
SUBJECT	ACHIEVEMENT	EFFORT	REMARKS
MATHS	F-	A+	Can count on his fingers, even with his hands in his pockets. However, he will insist that 5+5 = 11.
ENGLISH	F-	A+	Does a lot of reading – although I'm not convinced that 'Alice's Adventures in Rubber' or 'A Tale of Bristol Cities' will stand him in very good stead for the O-level exams.
GEOGRAPHY			
BIOLOGY ENVIRONMENTAL STUDIES	–	–	Banned from classroom for moaning during Reproduction lesson.
MUSIC ~~FRENCH~~	F-	E	Something is making him progressively deaf
HISTORY			
POTTERY ~~SCIENCE~~	F-	E	CAUSED A NASTY ACCIDENT WHEN THE HAIR ON THE PALM OF HIS HANDS GOT CAUGHT IN THE COGS OF THE POTTERS WHEEL.

TERM MICHAELMAS

SUBJECT	ACHIEVEMENT	EFFORT	REMARKS
ART HANDICRAFTS	F−	E	Something is making him progressively blind.
GAMES	F−	A+	HAS ACHIEVED SOME ASTOUNDING THINGS WHILST WEARING BOXING GLOVES.
PHYSICAL EDUCATION	F−	F	SOMETHING IS MAKING HIM PROGRESSIVELY SMALLER.
RELIGIOUS INSTRUCTION	F−	A+	I'VE NEVER FOUND ANYONE SO ADEPT AT FINDING THE DIRTY BITS IN THE BIBLE. CHEERS LOUDLY EVERY TIME 'HARLOTS' OR 'FOOLISH VIRGINS' ARE MENTIONED.

GENERAL PROGRESS:

A good self-starter.
Roger came into the school a fine, upstanding youth and will leave a misshapen, stunted wreck; just like his father before him.
Nevertheless, he is very self-sufficient and can amuse himself for hours on end.

ATTENDANCE Often to be found under blankets with torch, amusing himself for hours on end.

FORM TEACHER'S SIGNATURE Mr Hat-Trick

HEAD TEACHER'S SIGNATURE Dr Frotter

PARENT'S SIGNATURE X – The mark of his inflatable rubber mother

WEDNESDAY DECEMBER 18TH

Dear Diary

And may I be the first to wish you the Compliments of the Season.

'Christmas is coming,
Bunter's very fat,
There's something very nasty
in Wimp Minor's hat.'

Yes, the Christmas spirit has arrived at Fishfriars Hall. . . and, as a result, all the staff were crawling round on their hands and knees, noisily perpetuating Billy Connolly's 'Diced Carrot Hypothesis'. . . This mysterious, crippling illness seemed to be linked to the taking of a special schoolmasters' elixir — we knew this much because it had 'Teachers' written on the side of the bottle. Matron reported the fact that Mr Hitler, the Games Master, was a victim of the illness — the symptoms were apparently that he had passed out and had 'delighted pupils'. The Head suggested that she had made a mistake and really meant 'dilated pupils', but Matron insisted that his pupils were delighted, because he couldn't make them do their usual thousand press-ups over broken bottles and barbed wire while he was having his stomach pumped. Good Will was upon us all in our dormitory. I fought him off, pretending that I had a girlfriend back home.

We had decided to make our dormitory look as

festive as possible. Cowardly Major, the dorm bully, had nailed Wimp Minor over the door and plugged him into the mains, so that all his extremities would light up — from a distance he looked like a giant five of diamonds. . . Isotope Minimus was also useful as a matching Christmas decoration. He was born just near Sellafield Nuclear Power Station, where his father worked, and consequently he glowed in the dark. We placed a little snow scene on both of his heads and he looked smashing.

We had managed to get hold of a copy of an Adult Advent Calendar for the dorm wall, but Squinter Binns had stretched out a trembling hairy palm, snatched it and is now studying it by torchlight under his bed-covers. Even with his boxing-gloves on he managed to open all the windows. . . and speaking of opening all the windows, in walked Methane Minor, and that's quickly what we did. Methane Minor turned out to have a unique skill — he was the only one of the chaps who could blow up balloons and sing 'Away In A Manger' at the same time. . . Apparently Old Ben Flasher, the school caretaker, was locking up later that night, burst a balloon by mistake, smelt something funny and, seeing no-one else in the room, kicked his dog. . .

Mr Flasher, with the full blessing of the Headmaster and all the school governors, had been dressing up in a long red robe and a false beard, giving the first form boys sweets and bouncing them up and down on his knee — something which he had been arrested for back in August. . . I suppose that's just one of life's little ironies, as pater once said when mater caught him strutting round the house, dressed in her high heels and undies.

Capitalist-Swine Major had set up a stall selling exclusive Andy Warhol abstract Christmas cards for £2 a time — which turned out to be folded pieces of Corn Flakes box...

Wedgwood Bill and Benn Minor, the school looney, had written 'Santa's Grotto' on his top lip and was charging 50 pence a time for guided tours of his mouth...

Inside the grotto, Wedgwood Bill and Benn Minor had installed an ultra left-wing reindeer called Rolf, which had a Conservative-Detecting-Ray built into its nose. When the ray detected a passing Tory, Rolf reared up on his back legs and exposed himself... Yes, dear appalled at the contrived nature of it all Diary — it was... 'Red Rolf the ray-nosed rude deer...'

And sometime before dawn in my shockingly shatterproof sheets I wonder if the Games Master gets himself back to normal with a course of exercise and Sanatogen... will it be yet another triumph of Gym 'N' Tonic...?

And, during the Christmas celebrations, will the Headmaster discover Matron's dark secret, or will he go on believing that she's a natural blonde?

Lose a stone in three days
YES! JUST TWO DAYS
with

METHANE MINOR'S

F-PLAN DIET

Exclusive to readers of this book (and anybody else in the world we can get to show the slightest interest)...

We will send you the complete details absolutely free on receipt of just one cheque for £10.00
Rush your cheque for £12.00 now to:

SLIMMALONG-A-MEETH
POOH CORNER
WINDRUSH

Here is a mouth-watering extract from Day One of Methane's Revolutionary Diet:

BREAKFAST
One Ryvita
Prune Juice (Three pints)
Chicken Biryani
Mushroom Bhaji
Buttered Prawn Dupiaza
1 lb Marrowfat Peas
Guinness (11 pints)
(You may throw the Ryvita away)

LIGHT LUNCH
Mulligatawny Soup with floating Marrowfat Peas
Baked Beans on two thin slices of toast
Golden Lamb Pasanda with Marrowfat Peas
Marrowfat Peas served on a bed of Golden Lamb Pasanda
Pasanda in a Golden Lamb and Marrowfat Peas Sauce
Syrup of Figs (4 pints)
Mixed Pickles (2 jars)
Guinness (16 pints)
(If you are finding it heavy going, throw away the two thin slices of toast)

HIGH TEA
Beef and Mutton Dhansak
Mushroom Patia with Mushy Peas
Curried Beans with Currants
Mixed Pickles (5 jars)
Three glasses of hot cabbage water
Guinness (Half pint)
Guinness (18 more pints)

SUPPER

One Marrowfat Pea Sandwich

Fig, Pea and Mushroom Curry, with a Brussel Sprout side order

Chicken Patia stuffed with Sprouts, Mushrooms, Peas and Figs

Baked Beans (2 catering packs)

Mulligatawny Soup (5 litres)

Mixed Pickles (one supermarket shelf)

Mushy Peas and Beansprouts (1 cwt)

Rhubarb and Custard (1 bucket)

Guinness (1 crate)

SUGGESTED EXERCISE ROUTINE

Running and Sprinting: This will probably be involuntary, although any records broken will almost certainly be rejected as wind-assisted. In any case it's unlikely that any timekeeper would stay in the same stadium, or even the same country.

Pumping Iron: This is an inevitable but only temporary side-effect.

After supper suggested VIDEOS include: Jaws; Alien; The Chainsaw Massacre; and Wind In The Willows.

Rush £18 now to SLIMMALONG-A-MEETH

DON'T DELAY, SEND TODAY

FRIDAY DECEMBER 20TH

Hallo Dear Festive Diary

Today was the day of the Fishfriars Christmas Dinner: And what a spread it was dear drooling Diary. . . Mock Turtle Soup made out of Wimp Minor's pet tortoise, which we found hibernating under his bed. It obviously wasn't exactly the Mike Yarwood of the tortoise world, because it didn't mock turtles particularly well — although it did a very fair impression of a scabby donkey.

This was followed by a one thou' slice of turkey, carefully shaved off the bird by the woodwork master, Mr Spokeshave, with an extremely sharp plane. This was so that one stunted, scrawny 7lb. turkey, that the Headmaster had run over the previous day, could be divided between 842 of us. The only reason he had managed to run that one over was because it only had one leg, so drumsticks were a bit thin on the ground as well.

The gossamer-thin shaving of turkey was served with sprouts that had been boiled vigorously for 3½ weeks, in order to render them down to an appetising greeny-brown steaming sludge, not un-reminiscent of a fresh cow-pat, and raw potatoes with so many eyes that I felt as though I was being watched all through the meal. Dr Frotter, the Headmaster, took charge of flaming the Christmas pudding.

FRIDAY DECEMBER 20TH

Unfortunately, Sparky Butane, the school arsonist, had put 4-star petrol in the 4-star brandy bottle. When the Head appeared, the bottle was mysteriously half empty. He denied having drunk any, although we all had our suspicions — for a start he wasn't normally cross-eyed. . . and when he actually came to ignite the liquor on the pudding, he belched loudly and cremated the entire first form.

It being almost the end of the Christmas term, Mr Monopod, the one-legged Latin Master, was busy organising the School Hop. There was a great buzz of excitement when it was announced that dancing partners would be laid on. There was an even bigger buzz of excitement when Libido Major was actually caught lying on one, but that's another story. . .

Yes! As well as the handful of our own sixth form girls, who had all been snapped up by the staff weeks ago anyway, they were bringing in a party from the local girls' school for us to maul on the dance floor. On the side of the bus it said. . . 'Feels on Wheels'. . .

The Hop itself was great fun. A traditional tribal ritual was re-enacted — the girls formed a circle round a huge mountain of handbags and swayed to the music, while us chaps nonchalantly stood in clusters, pretending we were just about to dance with one of them and lying outrageously about previous sexual conquests. Cowardly Major, our dormitory bully, volunteered to act as doorman to the Dance Hall. He went missing though for 20 minutes while he took Mr Ageing-Hippy, the Art Master, outside to give him a good kicking for wearing jeans.

Squinter Binns had forsaken his dirty books and his

torch for the night, donned a huge mac and was walking round with a mirror on a stick, suspender-spotting.

Our top Latin scholar — Vesuvius Minor — won the Spot prize — for a cluster of real beauties on his chin and a huge boil on his nose.

Even old Ben Flasher, the school caretaker, had come to join in the fun, but had to be chucked out again during the 'Hokey-Cokey' when the Headmaster saw what he was putting in and shaking all about. . . Suddenly it was announced that it was 'Cabaret-Time'. Houdini Minor announced that he was going to undertake the most breathtaking escape ever performed. He was handcuffed to Methane Minor, the ever-flatulent fifth former, then padlocked and chained into a large wooden chest with him.

We all fell silent, holding our breath in sympathy, knowing how many plates full of sprouts Methane Minor had eaten at lunchtime. Suddenly we heard a low resonant rumbling and, within five seconds, Houdini Minor had bitten through the handcuffs, frantically clawed his way through the 1 inch plywood walls of the chest and ran screaming from the Hall, never to be seen again.

The climax of the cabaret came when Wimp Minor, with his suit on fire, dived 50 feet out of the window into the school compost heap. He hadn't particularly wanted to do it, but Cowardly Major can be very persuasive when he's got a chainsaw in his hand.

We had a smashing night, until one of the girls said she'd seen a peeping-tom up the drainpipe at the ladies' window. We all armed ourselves with the left-over cream cakes and custard pies and tried flicking them at him with lengths of rubber tubing. The only one though who made a direct hit was Clever-Dick Major who first spent ages properly coiling the rubber tubing. The moral of this painful parable is. . . 'He who pies the peeper, coils the tube.'

As I lie in my revolting recliner I think. . . 'Is it true that the new boy is the son of one of the greatest peers in the land — and will he be able to beat the school record of 7′6″ up the lavatory wall?'. . . and. . . 'Was Cowardly Major, the Dormitory Bully, responsible for throwing a 'water-bomb' full of Domestos at the School Chaplain during Sunday prayers — and will he be arrested for causing a bleach of the priest?'

Mr Spokeshave, the woodwork master, demonstrates the best way to avoid National Service, in the event of the reintroduction of conscription.

GLOSSARY OF USEFUL FISHFRIARS HALL PUPILS' EXPRESSIONS

"CRIPES!" An exclamation of surprise (e.g. when being struck over head with cricket bat).

"CRIKEY!" An exclamation of horror (e.g. upon discovering that the *News Of The World's* 'Transvestite Tory And Pillar Of Local Church Implicated In Shock Nunnery Vice Case' is none other than one's own dear pater. Or upon having parts of one's anatomy slammed in a desk-lid).

"CRUMBS!" An exclamation of bewilderment (e.g. upon accidentally stumbling into the girls' dormitory when Parton Maximus is unloading her tungsten-steel reinforced bra).

"ARCH-BEAKO" One of the few printable nicknames for Dr Frotter, the Headmaster. (Others refer to his alleged lack of male parentage, the resemblance of his head to various parts of the human anatomy, etc).

"I'M UP FOR A WHOPPING"

I've been summoned to have my human rights infringed by a sadist with an offensive weapon.

"A CORDUROY BOTTOM"

The results of having one's human rights infringed by a sadist with an offensive weapon.

"I SAY YOU CHAPS!"

An exclamation of displeasure (e.g. when the other chaps are filling your undies with molten lead, or kneecapping you with a pick-axe handle).

"YAROO!"

An exclamation of discomfort (e.g. when being interrogated with rubber hoses and a stocking full of sand at the local police station, for suspected apple-scrumping).

"A ROTTER"

A loathsome, pin-headed, rubber-faced, fat-necked, spotty illegitimate son of a doggy-do.

"A BLIGHTER"

Someone who has done one a disservice (e.g. coaxed your tortoise out of its shell with a sharp stick).

TUESDAY DECEMBER 24TH

Dirar Yuletide Deary

Christmas Eve today, and at Fishfriars Hall tradition said that we should put on a Nativity Play in the school gymnasium. Mr Leon Shirt-Lifter, the drama teacher, had been going around with his collection of compromising photographs, persuading us to take part in the play.

Casting had proved to be very difficult — I mean! You try to find three wise men in a public school! Capitalist-Swine Major was chosen to play King Herod and had already started preparing for the Herod's January Sale. . . he was also busy taking out Life Insurance Policies on all the male babies in the Bethlehem postal district.

Wimp Minor was a natural for the Virgin Mary, since none of the handful of sixth form girls met all the script requirements — not a Mary among them. Wimp Minor was perfect — he even had the blue dress, which he'd been making when everyone else was doing metalwork. When it came to the dress rehearsal, Leon Shirt-Lifter gave the young Wimp a medicine ball, with which to fake the pregnancy. Cowardly Major, with his trusty sink plunger, helped him to swallow the heavy ball — although we all felt it would have been much easier to just stick it up his jumper.

Prince Luko, being the youngest member of the

Royal Family, insisted on being one of the three kings, and Bunter, the disgusting fat pig of the Lower Remove, was to be the other two. A battle immediately started over who was going to bear the gifts — the gold, myrrh, or Frankie Says very little T-shirt. The big night had arrived. A stage had been built out of wooden tea-chests.

The parents all crowded in — Prince Luko's mater and pater caused quite a stir by insisting on sitting in one of the tea-chests, half-way up the wall-bars on the right-hand side of the gym', so that they could wave to everyone else. We all had to stand and sing 'God save Luko's mum' and then the play started with a regal fanfare on the toilet paper and comb.

I was playing Joseph and I led on the ass which was carrying Mary. The front end of the ass was Methane Minor. . . and who had drawn the short straw for the back end? — Yes, Squinter Binns had agreed to do it, providing that he was allowed to take some dirty books and a torch inside the skin with him. The twisted little chap's humpty-back made the ass look more like a camel, but no-one else could be made to cling to the lethal shirt-tail for an hour and a half, so he kept the part. For safety's sake, Methane Minor had been denied his favourite foods — mushy peas and sprouts — and he had been warned by the Headmaster that if he didn't control himself, he'd be in hot water. . . to which some wit observed that Methane Minor in hot water would make a good Jacuzzi. . . The heavily pregnant Wimp Minor in his blue dress and halo wobbled precariously as the strange beast lumbered across the make-shift stage.

And lo it came to pass that we didst all gather round the crib while Cowardly Major took Wimp Minor backstage, picked him up by the ankles and thumped him relentlessly until he coughed up the medicine ball, and then led him out again with real tears in his eyes, nursing his teddy bear wrapped in swaddling clothes.

Capitalist-Swine Major was busy pulling off the greatest con trick in recorded history — he was selling the rights to the exclusive story of the newborn baby to *four* different journalists — Matthew, Mark, Luke and John.

Suddenly, chaos reigned. Thatcher Major's fancy man Dennis the Thorough Menace School Buffoon and Phone Box Flooding Champion, was to play the angel Gabriel's herald. He hiccoughed loudly, causing his halo to slip down over his eyes — the sudden shock made one of the little lambs relieve itself on one of the shepherds. . . A tea-chest creaked and groaned and finally gave way under Bunter's enormous weight, sending him crashing through the stage. Methane Minor, seeing all this through the head of the ass, got a sudden fit of the giggles, which in turn caused him to lose his own self-control — the whole ass's skin inflated grotesquely for a few moments. . . poor old Squinter Binns made a muffled cry for help, the ass doubled-up convulsively, tore its skin in half, and the rear-end hurtled off into the night. . .

Wimp Minor burst into tears, his big scene ruined. . . Prince Luko noticed that his mater had sloped off to rearrange the words of her previous messages to the Commonwealth ready for the next day, so he sneaked out the back way with a handful of debutantes and

Sloane groupies who wanted to make the best of the opportunity, knowing that they wouldn't be getting any Royal Male over the Christmas period. . .

Cowardly Major saw an opportunity for some gratuitous bullying, ripped his wings off and started lacing seven bells out of the shepherds. The terrific din startled all the other lambs into making a shocking mess on the stage. Wimp Minor, alias Mary, tried to flee the stage, but slipped and fell full-length in the sheep dung. . . Poor old Leon Shirt-Lifter was so horrified by this deafening uproar that he lit one of his funny fat cigarettes and started giggling to himself with his eyes all glazed over. . . Yes, dear patient diary, it was a case of. . . 'Din, Dung on Mary, Leon high. . .'

As I lie in my flatulence-damaged flea-pit, I wonder whether Squinter Binns, the school pervert, spends so much time under his blankets with a torch because he wants to be an usherette when he grows up. . .

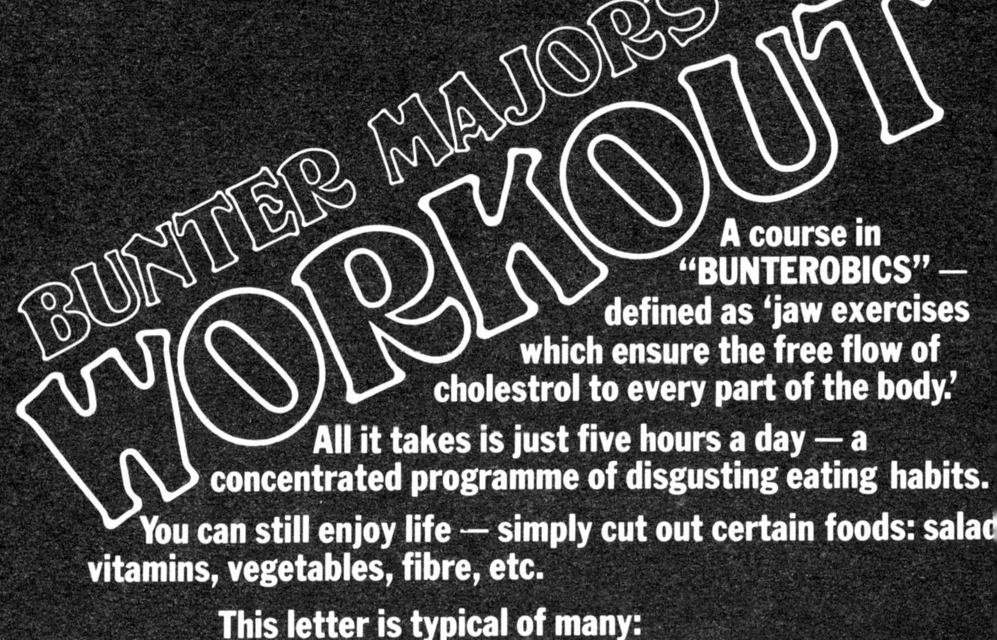

BUNTER MAJOR'S WORKOUT

A course in "BUNTEROBICS" — defined as 'jaw exercises which ensure the free flow of cholestrol to every part of the body.'

All it takes is just five hours a day — a concentrated programme of disgusting eating habits.

You can still enjoy life — simply cut out certain foods: salad vitamins, vegetables, fibre, etc.

This letter is typical of many:

> Dear Bunter Major
>
> I have been feeling a bit under the weather recently and I heard a doctor on TV say that you should alter your diet to one high in fibre and iron. It doesn't work!! . . . I have just spent three days eating a well-sprung settee . . . and would you believe it?? I now feel worse!!
>
> Yours sincerely
>
> Samuel Springtummy, Blackheath.

If you haven't the will-power to adopt gluttony as a way of life on your own, why not join your local KEEP-FAT CLASS?? — They'll pop you on a Heavy-Goods-Vehicle weighbridge once a week and they cheer and clap at every stone you put on . . . and 'B if you should let everyone down by losing weight one week.

The L.P. or cassette contains songs to help you to 'Eat To The Beat,' by well-known International fatties like: 'Meatloaf,' 'Demis Roussos,' 'The Weather Girls,' etc. with Bunter Major, the disgusting fat pig of the Lower Remove, offering words of encouragement, like:

"When you've eaten your dinner and could still eat a bag of chips — go for it! If you fancy a pound bar of chocolate, get up and — go for it! Guzzle down your dinner while it's still boiling- hot — Go for the burn!"

WEDNESDAY JANUARY 1ST

The school holidays seem to be going on for ever. . . The family was just sitting down to a hearty snack of turkey-burgers, turkey trifle and grilled lobster surprise — the surprise was that it wasn't really lobster, it was turkey!

We've almost eaten half of the damned bird by now, which pater swears was in fact a Matthews self-basting Norfolk Ostrich — which would explain why it buried its head in the mashed spuds when we tried to carve it.

All this over-eating is taking its toll. My Uncle Robert, a retired Chief Constable, has developed a spare tyre — which he said he was convinced was going to make a major contribution to his back-pocket when he started doing television adverts. . .

My school chums have put on weight too. Bunter Minor, younger brother of the disgusting fat pig of the Lower Remove, is having to go on a crash diet, because he'd eaten so much he couldn't get through the door-frame and was trapped in his parents' dining-room. They'd wired his jaws together to enforce his diet, but the crafty swine had been caught cramming cream buns up his nose and with a sherry trifle drip going into his right arm.

Cowardly Major, our dormitory bully, gained 17

pounds over Christmas — he'd mugged the Avon-lady.

Yes, we've all gained weight over the hols due to over-indulgence. . . Except, that is, for the handful of chaps who'd stayed back at Fishfriars Hall over Christmas, being looked after by our ever-lusty Matron — they've all lost stones, their pathetic little bodies all scrawny and wasted, through over-indulgence of quite a different kind. Matron assured their parents that they would be in capable hands. . . and by all accounts the rest of her turned out to be pretty accomplished as well.

New Year's Eve was a fairly miserable affair. Mater and pater went to a dinner-dance. Mater went dressed as a mermaid sitting on a huge plate covered with little cuddly toy monkeys. I asked her what she was supposed to be, to which she replied, 'Fish and Chimps!'. . . Pater, on the other hand, went as a drag-car racer — in a lovely powder-blue frock with matching shoes, handbag and crash-helmet.

Apparently their costumes caused quite a stir at the dance. . . mainly I think, because it wasn't Fancy Dress.

They left me as they did most years with a really boring baby-sitter. Last year it was a woman who was so old I had to take her up to the toilet and put her to bed. This year it was our next-door-neighbour's boring Swedish au pair girl, Inger. Every time I tried to settle down to watch Moira Anderson and Kenneth Mackellar on TV, she kept butting in with stupid suggestions of playing a boring card game — 'Strip Poker' I think she called it. . .

Then I was just trying to glean a few wrinkles on the

finer points of Scottish dancing and accordion-playing when she started making a nuisance of herself again — panting and reckoning something about her brassiere being too tight, and could I just unclip it for her. . .

No wonder it was uncomfortable — silly little black lacy thing with no ends in the cups, not a bit like the ones I'd seen pater trying on when mater was out shopping.

An hour and a half it took me to master that stupid brassiere clip, with her moaning the whole time. . . Then, of all the ungrateful things — the minute I'd got it unfastened for her she whispered in my ear — 'Bed!' — I said, 'No fear! I'm stopping up to watch the Bagpipe Band of the Scottish Dragoon Guards. This is New Year's Eve, I'm going to have fun!'

Methane Minor, the ever-flatulent fifth former, entered a sponsored baked beans eating contest and then spent New Year's Eve in the middle of Trafalgar Square — absolutely alone! He got drunk and sat in the fountain, singing 'I'm For Ever Blowing Bubbles'.

Prince Luko, youngest member of the Royal Family, spent New Year's Eve with his mater and the rest of the family, trying to work out who all the nondescript dogs-bodies were on Mrs T's New Year's Honours List and wondering if it had been a 'pin-in-the-phone-book-job'. . .

Cowardly Major spent the evening wandering around Sloane Square trying to find out where there was a posh dance going on — 'Spot The Ball' he called it. . . When he found a suitably big house, which in fact belonged to a High Court Judge called Justice Once, with a party going on he gate-crashed it. . . Then he door-crashed it. . . and then he crashed down the hall smashing all the ornaments. When it got to midnight and all the guests joined hands for 'Auld Lang Syne', he connected one of them up to the mains and wiped out the lot in a flash. . .

He himself sang two choruses of 'Should auld acquaintance be given a damned kicking?' and then ransacked the house.

In the judge's bedroom he found his little mallet, or 'gavel' as they are known, and used it to kneecap their large family of pedigree Siamese cats. Cowardly Major kindly offered to let one of the few survivors of his massacre, a young Sloane, have a turn at hitting the poor moggies with the gavel, but he declined, groaning in pain at his own injuries. . . which just goes to prove dear daily-more-despairing diary, that. . . 'a groaning Sloane gavels no mogs. . .'

And just as I nod off into the Little Land of Peepy Nigh Nights, I ponder — Is it true that when Mr McTavish, the Metalwork Master, was asked to do something traditionally Glaswegian for last year's Hogmanay celebrations, he was sick in a shop doorway??

And is there any truth in the rumour that the man who mucks out the school pigs went away to Brighton last week with a lady chimney-sweep in a dustbin-wagon for an extremely dirty weekend??

APPROXIMATE TRANSLATIONS OF COMMON PHRASES USED BY THE STAFF OF FISHFRIARS HALL

WHAT THEY SAY	WHAT THEY REALLY MEAN
In The Classroom	
'Come out here boy and tell all the class what you've written.'	You are an under-achiever and no threat to my faultering ego, therefore I'm going to make a complete fool of you in front of your friends.
'Because I say so boy!'	I don't know the reason either.
'You boy! Stand up! Stand on your chair so that we can all see how stupid you are!'	I fancy you something rotten you little tease.
'This afternoon we are going to sit in silence and revise!'	I'm too drunk to stand up at the blackboard.
On The Playing-Field	
'You boy! You idle wretch! You've flagged behind all the way round the Cross-Country Course! You will go back and run 50 times round the field, then I'll thrash you!'	Mother Nature has drawn the short straw on your behalf and has made you the fattest boy in the class.
To Parents On Open Days	
'Could do better.'	I'm not absolutely certain which one your son is.
'Average.'	I haven't a clue which one your son is!
'With a little extra private tuition, your boy could excel in my subject.'	I understand you're extremely rich.

TUESDAY JANUARY 7TH

Whoopee Dear Diary

Ra! Ra! Ra! It was back to school! There was much excited giggling and whooping — not from me, that was from mater and pater, who couldn't wait to see the back of me. Come to think of it, there were a couple of prefects who couldn't wait to see the back of me either, but that was quite another story. It was always one of the hardest things about going back to school, getting back into certain habits — like walking backwards when you're being followed by Gender-Bender Major, and remembering to padlock your trousers before going anywhere near the Sixth Form Common Room.

I stood at the school gates and drank in the sight which met my eyes — then I was sick! I'd drunk the school duck-pond!

I always get a tingle down my spine whenever I walk through the school gates — the wretched things are electrified and I always forget!

Nothing seemed to have changed at Fishfriars. Cowardly Major, our dormitory bully, had already slaughtered his first junior of the New Year. He had challenged the poor young chap to a duel of honour and had asked him to choose his favourite weapon — he had chosen boxing-gloves. . . unfortunately for him, Cowardly Major chose a machine-gun and mowed him down before he'd even tied the laces. . .

TUESDAY JANUARY 7TH

Gender-Bender Major trying desperately to explain away the ladies' undies his Mater has just found hidden under his bed.

Methane Minor was standing completely alone, eating a bag of sprouts, his grey flannels billowing ominously and the birds dropping like stones from the skies above him.

Our lusty Matron smiled an extremely contented smile as she unlocked the doors and let out the young chaps she had been taking care of during the hols. They blinked blindly in the bright winter sunlight and their shrivelled, withered bodies limped out into the playground. It was a known fact that if you went into Matron's room a boy, you came out a gibbering, dribbling old man with a bad back.

TUESDAY JANUARY 7TH

At the start of our first assembly of this new term in the Great Hall, the Chairman of the Board of Governors said he was afraid that he had something to spring on us. . . It turned out to be a rare silver mountain-lion, which sprang on us and ripped out the throats of several chaps who had pushed their way to the front of the Hall to see if they could see the new nurse's stocking-tops. Eventually the raging lion was subdued with a tranquiliser dart, normally reserved for use on chaps who had seen the nurse's stocking-tops.

The stunned silver mountain-lion was taken to the sick-bay where it could be tenderly revived by our animal-loving Matron. The bleeding mauled boys were told to pull themselves together or they would be severely flogged. . .

We were then all given an even bigger shock — over the holidays, Dr Frotter, our headmaster, had been involved in a misunderstanding involving a Tory M.P., a French loaf, a wet-suit, a jar of Swarfega, and 13 members of an unnamed youth organisation. . . and was being detained by Her Majesty.

Presumably he'd popped round to collect Prince Luko's school fees and she must have asked him to stay. . . although I have to confess, I never knew that she had a place in Brixton. . .

Anyway, as a result, we were going to have a temporary stand-in headmaster for a while. . . and, going by the state of the school, we all knew what he'd be standing in!. . .

Our new temporary headmaster, Mr Do-Gooder, was introduced to us. He was wearing a baggy brown corduroy suit and a CND badge. He admitted that, because he had been an SDP Alliance candidate he had great difficulty pronouncing the letters 'R' and 'L'. . .

'Yes,' he said, 'You pwobably won't be able to tell my 'R's from my 'L's boys. . .'

He then went on to tell us that he was a pwogwessive headmaster, which naturally meant that he was a gwaduate from the University of Cloud-Cuckoo-Land and a 'Save the Whale' campaigning vegetarian. As such, he announced that at meal-times, there would be no meat served — instead we were to eat Macdonald's burgers and British Rail pork pies. . . He also said that he was totally opposed to all forms of physical punishment and he was abolishing them immediately. A huge cheer went up round the Hall. . . then a huge cloud of smoke went up as well, as everyone lit a celebratory cigarette. Mr Do-Gooder told them to put them out at once. 'Or else what will you do??' echoed round the Hall from two hundred pairs of synchronised lips. . . 'Or else I'll get vewy vewy cwoss!' lisped Mr Do-Gooder. It was said that the ensuing laughter could be heard 15 miles away in the next valley. . .

Cowardly Major took advantage of the sudden lack of discipline and began force-feeding Wimp Minor with a pile of Hymn Books and then attempted to unscrew his head. Mr Do-Gooder stood aghast, looking at the young Wimp's tortured, groaning body and then turned and said, 'Cowardly Major, you poor child, I can see that you have a problem — take a week off school!'. . .

Naturally enough, for the next ten minutes, the Hall

rang with screams and the crunch of boot meeting bone as all the larger boys kicked seven bells out of the juniors, in order to earn an extra week's holiday. . . Meanwhile, large groups of pupils were leaving the Great Hall to play cards, have snowball fights, and make snowmen. . . Of course dirty little Squinter Binns made a snow-woman and seemed to spend an unnecessary length of time sculpting certain areas. . . The poor Mr Do-Gooder was almost at the end of his tether, with the pupils all fighting or playing in large unruly crowds, when suddenly he received even worse news. The rare silver mountain-lion had escaped, rounded up all its mates and they had split up such that one lion was attacking each group of boys — yes, dear hardly-daring-to-breathe Diary. . . 'Every crowd had a silver lion in. . .'

This evening as I lie back on my maggot-riddled mattress, I wonder whether Cowardly Major will spend his week off sitting in a corner with a magnifying glass and a little toffee hammer, patiently kneecapping a centipede?

THURSDAY FEBRUARY 6TH

Dear Singlet-and-tights-clad Diary

Hello again. Today was a big day in the school calendar — we'd got a cheap batch of reject calendars where the pages are all different sizes, and today's was a real whopper!! It was also an important day for our Drama Teacher, Mr Shirt-Lifter. It was the day when the men dress up as women and the women get their thighs slapped. No! Not The Board of Governors' AGM, it was the school pantomime. . . Ohhh yes it was!!!

Of course the first problem had been to decide which pantomime to do. Mr Shirt-Lifter said he fancied 'Aladdin'. We'd guessed as much, but fancied a lad in what?? A lad in rubber shorts?? A lad in leather jodhpurs?? A lad in custard??? In the end we decided to have a bash at 'Cinderella'. Mr Shirt Lifter started the casting session while we were eating tea one night. Suddenly one of my sandwiches got up, walked to the end of the table, and took a bow — Yes, dear tortured Diary, I'd been given an 'acting roll'. . . The demented butty strutted up and down, trying to do a speech from 'Macbeth', but went way over the top — but then of course dear even-more-tortured Diary, it was a *ham* sandwich. . .

'Who else wants to be in the pantomime?' asked Mr Shirt-Lifter. 'I want to be Cinders!' trilled dear little Wimp Minor — so Cowardly Major set fire to him.

FISHFRIARS HALL SCHOOL REPORT

NAME	Melvyn Wimp (Wimp Minor)		
SUBJECT	ACHIEVE-MENT	EFFORT	REMARKS
MATHS	F-	F-	When we do 'vulgar fractions', he blocks his ears and hums loudly, so as not to listen.
ENGLISH			
GEOGRAPHY			
BIOLOGY ENVIRONMENTAL STUDIES	F-	F-	Fainted when we examined the inside of a daffodil, and begged to be excused Sex Education Classes, as he felt sick as soon as we'd got to 'holding hands'.
FRENCH	F-	F-	Has the annoying habit of insisting on saying 'TINKLES' as the French translation of the word 'YES'
HISTORY			
GARDENING ~~SCIENCE~~	F-	F-	FOUND A HEDGEHOG UNDER A GOOSEBERRY BUSH, AND INSISTS IT'S HIS SON.

TERM *Spring*

SUBJECT	ACHIEVEMENT	EFFORT	REMARKS
ART HANDICRAFTS	F-	A+	Banned from Art room for painting a pair of trousers and a vest on my favourite print of 'The Birth of Venus'.
GAMES PHYSICAL EDUCATION	A+	F-	RUGBY - MELVYN IS EXTREMELY USEFUL IN THE SCRUM - WE WRAP HIM UP IN A WASH-LEATHER AND USE HIM AS THE BALL
RELIGIOUS INSTRUCTION	F-	F-	CROSSES HIMSELF SHOUTING, "GET THEE HENCE SATAN!" AT ME EVERY TIME I TALK ABOUT 'THE FOOLISH VIRGINS' - WHICH IS MOST ANNOYING, WHAT WITH YOUNG BINNS CHEERING + WHISTLING, AND PRINCE LUKO ASKING FOR THIER PHONE NUMBERS

GENERAL PROGRESS:

Melvyn is the most snivelling, sycophantic, creeping, wet little "Toady" I've ever had the misfortune to teach. Has he ever considered becoming a TV Game Show Host?

ATTENDANCE *200 Days Absence due to "Pernicious Dandruff"*

FORM TEACHER'S SIGNATURE *Mr Hat-Trick*

HEAD TEACHER'S SIGNATURE *Dr Frotter*

PARENT'S SIGNATURE *Arnold Wimp (Civil Service)*

THURSDAY FEBRUARY 6TH

Matron was hoping to be cast as 'Little Miss Muffet sat on a tuffet'. She said she wasn't bothered about having her curds with 'Buttons', but she was quite keen to have her whey with him.

Prince Luko, the none-too-bright youngest member of the Royal Family and next in line to be photographed in a night club with his trousers round his ankles, was given a token part as a deaf and dumb guest at Prince Charming's Ball. Apparently he couldn't sleep for days, worrying about learning his lines.

Two of the recently-admitted 6th form girls were cast as Prince Charming and Dandini — which prompted Squinter Binns to arm himself with a pair of greased surgical gloves and a couple of warm spoons, and volunteer to help the long-legged nymphets in and out of their snug-fitting singlets and thigh-boots.

When it came to the dress rehearsal Mr Shirt-Lifter had all sorts of problems. The pantomime donkey costume had arrived, but it had no eye holes, and the wearers kept falling off the stage. So a glass window had been fitted in the donkey's head — I think this is probably what's known — dear desperately-disclaiming-any-responsibility-whatsoever Diary — as a 'pane in the ass'.

Because of the small stage, Mr Shirt-Lifter had grumbled to the Set Designer that the Ballroom was very limited. . .

'Yes sir!' a voice chirped up from the back of the Hall, 'My trousers are a bit on the tight side too!'

The big night had arrived. The audience took their seats. . . we made them put them back again.

Cowardly Major, our dormitory bully, warmed the audience up — he set fire to the Great Hall! . . . and the curtain rose — which was odd as it usually went sideways. . .

Swotty Beaumont, the school boffin, brought the stage-lights up — which served him right for eating them in the first place. . . and Gender-Bender Major, as the Fairy Godfather, minced to the front of the stage and sang a rousing chorus of 'If I Were The Only Boy In The World, Mothercare Would Go Out Of Business'. . . and the panto was underway! The audience booed and hissed in all the appropriate places — come to think of it, they booed and hissed more or less all the way through.

The Pungent Sisters, played by Methane Minor and Stephen 'Sweaty' Swinton, came on stage — in fact Methane Minor floated on — his feet weren't touching the ground, and the combination of his long voluminous skirt and his 'F-Plan' eating habits had caused an effect reminiscent of the early hovercrafts — He span round, out of control several times, and then the sloping stage made him shoot forwards, until he crashed off the edge into the orchestra pit, where he came to rest, appropriately enough, in the Wind Section.

Squinter Binns was the prompter but, going by the deep breathing and the steam coming out of his ears, the book on his lap wasn't necessarily the pantomime script. This was confirmed when Wimp Minor, as Cinderella, asked what the next line was and Squinter huskily groaned something about 'milky-white thighs and firm jutting something-or-others. . .'

THURSDAY FEBRUARY 6TH

Wimp Minor on his way out for a night of unbridled fun and revelry.

The best bit was the magical scene. Wimp 'Cinderella' Minor wept bitterly in his fully automated, computerised kitchen and said, 'Woe is me! I'm sick of pressing buttons all day!' — so Buttons got off the ironing-table and sneered, 'We have fixed you, Cinderella! Your Pungent Sisters have gone to Prince Charming's Ball — well at least one of them has and the other will follow as soon as he gets his head out of the euphonium — and *you* will never get to meet the Prince!'.

With that there was a big 'puff' and in minced Gender-Bender again. 'Buttons! You are undone!'

'They most certainly are!' yelled Old Ben Flasher, the school caretaker, from the back of the Hall, standing on his seat and causing three women to pass out and thirty-five to get their opera glasses steamed up.

Gender-Bender continued undeterred, 'You shall go to the Ball!' and he performed the time-honoured magical transformation scene.

Thatcher Major and Heseltine Minor, the school Greaseball, aptly cast as a couple of rats, were turned into footmen. . . the pumpkin, which was of course really Fatty Bunter with his arms and legs sawn off, was turned into a coach — which was freezing cold, had ripped seats, and sick on the floor — yes, it was a second-class Inter-City coach.

All seemed to go well until the scene after the Ball where Prince Charming has to find whose foot fits into the broken bottle — well it was the nearest thing to a glass slipper we could find. The long-legged nymphet who was to have played the thigh-slapping prince had been offered a part as a cocaine-sniffing mass-murderer and exotic nude dancer with a tendency towards cannibalism, in the racier new-look 'Crossroads'. . . so, aptly, Prince Luko was given the part in her place. The trouble came when he had to try the bottle on the feet of The Pungent Sisters. . .

Stephen 'Sweaty' Swinton took one of his putrid boots off to reveal a horrible steaming, festering sock — the poor Prince was completely overcome. The curtain had to be brought down as he slumped unconscious over the noxious chap's smelly feet. . . Yes, dear long-suffering diary, 'Good Queen Windsor's Lad Passed Out On The Feet Of Stephen.'

THURSDAY FEBRUARY 6TH

As I lie under my daily deteriorating eiderdown, I wonder whose blankets Gender-Bender Major might sleep-walk under tonight. And if it's such an involuntary action, how come he always takes his curlers out and puts a little scent behind his ears before he sets off?

Squinter Binns at h
studies (note hair on pal
of hand)

CONFECTUS FLASHA
BRITANNICUS
"Take the Sweets and Think of England"
FISHFRIARS
HALL
SCHOOL
MENU

MENU

To Tickle The Palates of Young Gentlemen

MON-FRI: WEEK 12

Chef's notes will add to your enjoyment of these delights.

MONDAY

Opening Medicine

Thin Gruel

Honest Katkins Paté

Salt-Tack Bullets with a Tapioca side-order

Potatoes in their jackets

Rabbit à la Sir Robert Mark

(Freshly killed, with tyre-marks all over it. A major contribution to the Menu and I thoroughly recommend it.)

Semolina

Chocolate Sludge

TUESDAY

Opening Medicine

Much Thinner Gruel

Roast Hedgehog

(This is a male pig killed with kindness by having a complete PRIVET inserted up its back passage. Whichever pupil is lucky enough to get the snout will spot an unmistakable smile on its face.)

Mexicorn

(A selection of Lee Trevino's best golfing jokes, totally indigestable, but each boy must try.)

Potatoes in their trousers, and stuffed with Tapioca

Semolina

Chocolate Sludge

WEDNESDAY

Opening Medicine

Really Skinny Gruel

Chicken à la Jonathan King

(This has no real meat in it at all, it's filled with hot air, but it continues to make a high-pitched whining noise long after it's been certified as brain-dead.)

Parton Dumplings

(Two for each boy, and they'll be fired at each table in a giant elasticated catapult.)

St Bernard's Stew

(If the kennels are out of St Bernards on Wednesday we have been promised a breeding pair of free range Jack Russells.)

Potatoes in just their socks but keeping their ties on

Toad in the Hole

(This is a real toad run over by myself out hunting early in the morning for Rabbits à la Sir Robert Mark. There's no hole, as it's filled with Tapioca.)

Semolina

Chocolate Sludge

THURSDAY

Opening Medicine

Gruel Anorexia Nervosa

Electric Chicken

(This is a whole battery hen served complete with jump leads, and stuffed with currents. Best enjoyed standing on the table with both feet in a bucket of water.)

Bore's Head

(This dish may not be available if we can't get Ken Barlow to lie down on the scaffold for long enough.)

Turkey à la Walter Raleigh

(This is actually a potato stuffed with tobacco and eaten off a very muddy cape.)

Potatoes in the absolute nuddy

(This is best eaten with a hand over your eyes.)

Tapioca in a Semolina Sauce with a Chocolate Sludge side-order

Chocolate Sludge stuffed with Semolina, served on a bed of Frogs Spawn

(Sorry, no tapioca, but then we never use the real thing anyway.)

FRIDAY

Gruel Pegged Out

Dead Dog Stew on a Golden Bed of An Eka Rice

(The meat is absolutely awful but it does have a lovely bottom . . . and is dropped into the canteen from a helicopter.)

Venison Araby

(This is not actually Deer at all but Camel served in a plate absolutely swilling in oil and pound notes, served up in an old pair of Egyptian Taxi-Driver's Y-fronts.)

Chicken à la Long John Silver

(Only one leg per boy please, and a nasty taste of parrot.)

Potatoes not actually in the nuddy but wearing suspenders, a peek-a-boo bra and carrying a bullwhip

Kedgeree Surprise

(The surprise is that it's actually Semolina.)

Semolina Surprise

(The surprise is that it's actually Tapioca.)

Chocolate Sludge

Closing up again till Monday Medicine.

WEDNESDAY MARCH 5TH

Dour Diary

It was a peculiar day at Fishfriars Hall — our form did science all day long. We were making up for lost time as our Science Master, Mr Frankenstein, had just been released from prison following an unfortunate misunderstanding with the school sheep. . .

Mr Frankenstein began our marathon Science lesson by saying, 'First, boys, we will do Chemistry and the making of gases. . .'

'Yip'ee!' whooped Methane Minor, and dashed down to the school canteen to see if he could get himself a double helping of boiled cabbage. . .

Mr Frankenstein looked at Prince Luko, the youngest member of our Royal Family and third in line for all the jokes about big ears, and he said, 'Your Highness — if I took your crown and put it into hot concentrated nitric acid until it started frothing and dissolving, and I collected all the brown fumes that came off, what would I get?'

'Beheaded!' came the somewhat obvious reply. . .

He then demonstrated adding acid to Ferrous Sulphide which gave off Hydrogen Sulphide — the traditional 'rotten-eggs' stink-bomb gas.

The dreadful stench filled the whole laboratory, then crept under the door into the next room where our housemaster Mr Hat-Trick, or Jerry as we knew him, was teaching Latin. The poor old chap turned his nose up in horror, completely misread the situation and sent a boy with a creaking chair to be beaten by the Headmaster. . . Pretty soon the stinking gas had pervaded the whole school, which made Methane Minor come dashing out of the canteen, thinking that his family had arrived for a visit. . .

When the gas finally cleared, Mr Frankenstein went on to talk about the pressure cf gases, and demonstrated by pushing the drawer of a matchbox half way out. He then blew down the open end. . . of course the drawer flew out with the increased air pressure and hit the far wall. It didn't take long for Cowardly Major to discover that the same principle applied to the school tortoise.

We then turned to Physics. Mr Frankenstein said that anyone who knew one of the fundamental laws of Physics should stick their hands up. . . There was a startled squeal from one of the girls, and Furtive-Lust Major was given a hundred lines. . .

Wimp Minor, as usual, was the only one eager to answer a teacher's question — 'Please Sir! Me Sir! First Law of Physics Sir! — Matter can neither be created nor destroyed Sir'. . .

Cowardly Major turned round and said, 'Well, if that's true, you little toady, you won't mind if I set fire to your satchel!' — and he did just that. The poor little Wimp blubbered his heart out as he whined that his pencil case, his tuck and his pet slug were all destroyed in the blaze. . . 'That, according to your stupid law,' said Cowardly Major, 'is no matter. . .'

'What about the Laws Of Gravity?' asked Mr

Frankenstein. 'If I were to throw you up into the air, Cowardly Major, why would you come straight back down again?'. . . 'To give you a good kicking for taking liberties!' came the prompt reply.

Our dear teacher explained that what goes up must come down. . . 'Except mortgages!' gloated Capitalist-Swine Major.

Mr Frankenstein battled on — 'a massive body attracts a smaller body'. . . 'A bit like Fatty Boy George and Marilyn!' quipped Tarbuck Minor, the school show-off, who was so amused by his own joke that he had to be allowed to go back to the dorm to change.

A good teacher knows when he's beaten, so he hastily summed up by saying that absolutely everything obeys the laws of gravity, then suddenly he turned to the girls with a far-away look in his eyes and murmured 'Well perhaps I can think of a couple of exceptions!' Poor Parton Maximus blushed deep red, right up to the roots of her silly blonde wig. . .

Mr Frankenstein then announced that we would conclude our day of Science by doing Biology Practical. There followed another startled squeal from one of the girls, and Furtive-Lust Major was given a further hundred lines. He should have known better than to interfere with Selena Starchy-Pants, the school untouchable, who gets phenomenal amounts of spending-money for looking as though she never has, but might at any minute — and for flashing her legs at Breakfast-Time. (Bough Minor always calls her 'The Pools Queen', because she wears 'no-score-drawers'.)

Mr Frankenstein suddenly claimed that his

teaching notes on 'Reproduction' had been stolen and that he refused to continue the lesson until they were found. We traced the tell-tale sounds of asthmatic gasping to a small dark cupboard where we found smutty Squinter Binns studying the revelatory notes and explicit drawings of rampant rabbits by torchlight. . .

The poor chap had a fixation for months afterwards that he was abnormal and would never father children because he didn't have a white fluffy tail.

Eventually we got on with our Biology Practical and, by popular vote, we decided to dissect a frog. Aznavour Minor was none-too-chuffed as we pinned him to the dissecting board, but we looked on it as a service to music-lovers everywhere. . . Unfortunately Mr Frankenstein stopped us at the last minute, mumbling something about some ancestor of his that got into trouble for human experimentation.

We tried to explain that Aznavour Minor didn't really count as a human, but Mr Frankenstein insisted we stop and take a late lunch. To save time he sent Wimp Minor down to a well-known Fast-Food chain for a large pack of hamburgers. . . Poor old Aznavour Minor was still shaking so much from his ordeal that he said he could only face a plain buttered scone. . . So, dear punch-drunk diary, Mr Frankenstein's final instruction to Wimp Minor was. . . 'Get a Big Mac Party-Pack and give the frog a scone. . .'

As I lie in my evil-smelling pyjies tonight at Fishfriars I wonder, would it be more economical for the Government to keep Methane Minor in mushy peas, rather than keep drilling in the North Sea for Natural Gas.

FRIDAY MARCH 21ST

Another Lwerly Day Dear Dysentry

The morning sun was in the sky; the early birds had all caught worms; and the new-born gambolling lambs were all playing 5-Card Brag in a nearby field. . . It had all the makings of a perfect spring morning — until I was woken by a glancing blow with a supersonic building-brick. . . 'How dare you go to sleep in the middle of my lesson??!' yelled Mr Gadaffi, our Humanities Master. . . 'Sorry sir, I'll make sure I go to sleep at the back next time. . .' I quipped cheerily. . . Equally cheerily he hurled another brick, which only missed my right ear by a couple of inches — and smashed my nose to pulp! 'Take a hundred lines!' Mr Gadaffi said with a bark — I was quite surprised — he didn't usually do animal impressions.

Eventually the bell went. Someone was sent to look for it, and Mr Gadaffi menacingly whispered in my ear before leaving the classroom. The other chaps seemed somewhat amused to see me take out my heated rollers and start back-combing my hair in a 'bouffon' style, making it stand higher and higher, until I made Mari Wilson and Bet Lynch look like a pair of 'suede-heads'. How everyone laughed!. . . I was sure Mr Gadaffi had told me to 'beehive myself' after he had gone. . .

The morning passed all too quickly, because this afternoon our form were all to do a Cross-Country-Run for Mr Hitler, the amiable Games Master and arch-opponent of Corporal Punishment — himself preferring garrotting. . . The first mention of a Cross-Country-Run always filled the Sick Bay to overflowing with unlikely ailments like: 24 hour bubonic plague; tennis elbow; housemaid's knee; and Debutante's Ball.

Miserably, those of us who had failed to convince Mr Hitler we were terminally ill, changed into our shorts and plimsolls for the run. Mr Hitler, yelling about our scruffy turn-out, came up behind us and tried to snap off two pieces of white elastic hanging down from Wimp Minor's frayed baggy shorts. The poor little chap screamed the place down before any of us realised that 'the two pieces of elastic' were in fact his pale little legs. . .

All too soon we stood shivering by the school gates. The icy wind howling round the legs of our brief shorts had a devastating effect on Sprinkler Peabody, and the ever-thirsty little fellow disappeared as a huge cloud of steam engulfed him — local weathermen reporting him as a localised fog-bank moving rapidly round the Cross-Country course. . .

Wimp Minor was blown over by a freak gust of wind. Methane Minor, the ever-flatulent fifth former and chap voted least desirable person to be trapped in a lift with, was the freak responsible. . . By way of punishment, Mr Hitler made him lie face-down in the mud, with his right hand on one football, his left hand on another football, and do 100 press-ups. . . As some wit pointed out, he looked as though he was in training for a night out with Dolly Parton. . .

Mr Hitler then asked Tarbuck Maximus, the school show-off, to explain the route. . . 'It's the little white dangly thing at the bottom of a plant that grows down into the ground. . . Boom Boom. . ." he guffawed loudly. The funeral was a quiet, but tasteful affair. . .

The Cross-Country-Run was almost ready to start. The extreme right-winger Mr Hitler didn't want any chance of Baldy Kinnock being first past the winning-post this year, so he informed him that he had to carry his usual handicap — Wedgwood Bill and Benn Minor, the school looney.

The whistle blew and we were off! Old Ben Flasher, the school caretaker's were off too, but that's another story. . . As soon as we had gone a couple of hundred yards and disappeared round the corner of the Fishfriars Hall perimeter wall, we all collapsed in a wheezing, gasping heap. Cowardly Major, our dormitory bully, who had been surprisingly quiet up to now, suddenly leapt on Wimp Minor and, using his powerful talents of persuasion and equally powerful pincers to extract a few of Wimp Minor's toenails, persuaded the frail little weed to give him a piggy-back all the way round the course. Fortunately though, no sooner had Cowardly Major mounted poor little Wimp Minor's bony back, than a shocked dog ran out and threw a bucket of water over the pair of them. . .

Bunter Major, the disgusting fat pig of the Lower Remove, then decided that he too wanted a piggy-back — however we pointed out that he already had a piggy-front and a piggy-head, so he'd have to settle for that. . .

FRIDAY MARCH 21ST

Suddenly there was a bit of a rumpus as the Royal Sedan-Chair bearers went on strike and refused to carry their bejewelled and almighty leader round the 35 mile course, and poor Wogan Maximus had to get out and walk. But then he announced he could conjure up leprechauns in Ireland, so he was sure he could conjure up a fairy here in England to whisk him round the course. He gave Gender-Bender Major a fiver and demanded to be carried carefully round the course. Gender-Bender just looked down at his high-heeled shoes, went red and did nothing. How we all laughed. Eventually we could hold out no longer and all joined together in a rousing chorus of 'It's The Wrong Way To Tip A Fairy.'

This same evening, lying on my putrefying pillow, I wonder if Reagan Maximus the school prune will be the first past the winning post, his scrawny jowls billowing and his withered body perspiring heavily. . . and if so, would that mean the winner was a Turtle-Necked Sweater. . .?

FISHFRIARS HALL SCHOOL REPORT

NAME	Parton Maximum (Miss)		
SUBJECT	ACHIEVE-MENT	EFFORT	REMARKS
MATHS	46	C+	Her strength lies in the Statistics Department
ENGLISH			
~~GEOGRAPHY~~	A+	A+	On the last school trip she got many admiring glances around The Peak District.
BIOLOGY ENVIRONMENTAL STUDIES			
MUSIC ~~FRENCH~~	F-	F-	TONE DEAF WITH A WHINING TONELESS VOICE - HAS A GREAT CAREER AHEAD OF HER AS A COUNTRY & WESTERN SINGER.
COOKERY ~~HISTORY~~	A+	A+	Could win prizes with her dumplings.
SCIENCE			Very big in Human Biology! (Mind you, she's hardly Twiggy in Chemistry!)

TERM SPRING

SUBJECT	ACHIEVEMENT	EFFORT	REMARKS
~~ART HANDICRAFTS~~ DANCE	F-	F-	TOTALLY USELESS! ANYONE WOULD THINK SHE HAD DIFFICULTY SEEING HER OWN TWO FEET.
GAMES PHYSICAL EDUCATION	B-	A+	THERE ARE ONLY A COUPLE OF THINGS GET IN THE WAY OF HER BECOMING A PROFESSIONAL GYMNAST.
RELIGIOUS INSTRUCTION			

GENERAL PROGRESS:

What a lovely big fine girl! She comes into the staffroom to make tea and coffee for us all, and everyone agrees that she fills her cups to perfection

ATTENDANCE ____________

FORM TEACHER'S SIGNATURE Miss Brick Out-House

HEAD TEACHER'S SIGNATURE Dr Frottep

PARENT'S SIGNATURE Big Momma Parton

SATURDAY MARCH 22ND

Back Again Dear Diary

Sorry I didn't finish my entry yesterday, but I was so excited as I was writing it that I fell into a deep comatose sleep and cracked my head on the cast-iron bed-post. Sports don't seem to be one of the schools great strengths. Trouble is, nor does anything else.

Let me remind you where I'd got to, dear distraught Diary. Mr Hitler, our amiable Games Master and leader of our proposed trip to Poland, had sent us on a 35-mile Cross-Country Run and we had collapsed in a wheezing heap outside the school gates – after just 200 yards. What do you mean that's not much of a storyline??? — It would have taken 'East Enders' six weeks to get that far!

It was only when we noticed that the 6th Form girls had been sent for a run by their somewhat masculine, moustachioed Games Mistress, Miss Brick-Out-House, that we managed to pick ourselves up and, led by Benjamin Hill, the fat leering prefect and full time weirdo, gave chase at high speed. . .

Life at Fishfriars Hall had become more interesting ever since a handful of nubile nymphets had been introduced into the 6th Form as an experiment. . . I say 'a handful' — in fact Parton Maximus was more of a couple of policeman's helmets full! Watching her run past us was certainly a sight for sore eyes — and, by the end of the race, she'd not only have sore eyes, but fairly badly bruised knees as well!

As far as the girls' race went, Collins Major, the extremely Senior Girl who has had so much plastic surgery that if she stands too close to the fire she gives off toxic fumes, was the local bookie's favourite. . . She was also the local curate's favourite, and she was extremely well thought of by the entire 5th Regiment at the local Army Base.

Thatcher Major was also maintaining a strong challenge. The girls' initial fast pace was due to being set off by Old Ben Flasher, the school caretaker, who had lined them up and dropped the starter's flag — then he had dropped his boiler-suit and chased them down the drive wearing nothing but suspenders, black stockings and wellington boots. The frightened girls screamed and ran, not realising that he had in fact scratched himself from the race by hurdling over the hawthorn hedge and misjudging the height. It was four hours before the fire brigade managed to disentangle him, during which time he had broken the World Yodelling Endurance Record.

Furtive-Lust Major yelled, 'Let's follow the girls into the woods!'. . . 'Yes, yes!' chirped up Wimp Minor, 'Then we can all pick bluebells together!'. . . Cowardly Major, our dormitory bully, seemed to think this was as good a reason as any to push the naive little chap face down in a steaming cow-pat.

Dennis The Thorough Menace — Thatcher Major's Greek-God-like chaperone and freelance village idiot — said he wasn't going into the dark woods as he had lost his bottle. . . and he was going to retrace his staggering steps to look for it as he hadn't had a drink for almost five minutes.

The rest of us dived into the woods with gay abandon. . . However, gay Abandon took one look at the lusty girls and dived out again.

Meanwhile, the girls were selecting their prospective partners. . . Collins Major was weighing up the older boys — Nureyev Major won by a good 12½ ounces. . .

Parton Maximus slipped off her bulging sweater, thrust out her chest and asked if anyone was man enough to try it on. . . Wimp Minor tried it on and nearly suffocated!. . . 'Not the sweater!' she yelled frustratedly. . .

Prince Luko, youngest member of the Royal Family and latest in a long line of prolific ear-growing experts, was beginning to get into his stride with the girls. In true Royal style, he had very soon tried out every girl in the woods — and a flock of sheep in the next field were beginning to look decidedly worried.

Squinter Binns, the short-sighted stunted little wreck, was quite happy just to watch — his hairy palms allowing him to climb ape-like up the nearest tree. It wasn't for nothing that he had been dubbed 'The school Do-It-Yourself King'.

Suddenly, just as the wood was ringing with moaning and gasping, Mr Hitler and Miss Brick-Out-House yelled at us in unison. . . Collins Major's face fell — apparently the stitching at the back of her neck had gone — there was the rippling sound of unravelling skin and her face fell right down to her chest, which, in turn, fell to somewhere round her waist.

SATURDAY MARCH 22ND

Someone had shopped us!. . . We looked round and, sure enough, Iscariot Minor, the school sneak, was missing. . . Iscariot Minor was a real toady! I'll never forget after the Last Midnight Feast when he betrayed me to the prefects by kissing me on the cheek — I wouldn't have minded so much, but I was bending to tie my shoe lace at the time!

Sure enough we were all marched to school and severely punished — we were made to watch every episode of 'The Day My Underpants Changed' by James Utter-Burke, with our eyelids propped permanently open. . . Now it will come as no surprise to anyone who notices how totally contrived the rest of this is, that Jack Rosenthal, the famous playwright, just happened to be in the school at that time, doing research for his latest masterpiece. Unfortunately, because of our naughtiness, he was forbidden to talk to us boys — instead he had to sit with us and suffer the endless tedious hours of James Utter-Burke — which, as I am sure you've already realised, deer teeth-grinding diary, could only lead to one possible conclusion. . . 'All Burke and no boys makes Jack a dull play. . .'

As I half doze in my deplorably delapidated duvet sometime towards dawn, I find myself thinking: How will Methane Minor's parents react to their son's harsh punishment — will they come into school and make a stink?

NOTES ON MATRON's C.V.

Name: Fiona Mandy Rice Mata Hari Janie Jones Jezebel Keeler Richmond (also known as 'Madame X')

Current Occupation: School Matron, Fishfriars Hall

Age: Anybody's guess! (Admits to 33 summers...and a good number of years when it never seemed to get any warmer)

Marital Status: Anybody's! (Seeks wealthy middle-aged businessman for daytime outings and activities, and professional rugby team for night-time activities)

Education: Passed Advanced Level 'Doctors and Nurses' in school bike sheds at the 'Lady Chatterly Academy For Mixed Infants'
Majored in 'Mothers and Fathers' behind cricket pavilion at 'The Fanny Hill Secondary Modern'
Undergraduate research at The University of Sodom and Gomorrah (Claims to have spent more time under graduates than Mrs Robinson - 'purely in the interests of research, you understand')

Career: While still at University took evening job as exotic dancer in order to sponsor three-man team of experts to explore the Erogenous Zones.
World Mud-Wrestling Champion for eleven glorious years. Used to intimidate opponents by scouring the mud for worms before the commencement of each bout and eating them in the middle of the ring.

Became Army Nurse and Masseuse. Responsible single-handed for the Relief of Mafeking. (Mafeking extremely grateful)

World 'How-Far-Can-You-Kick-Russell-Harty-Over-A-Rugby-Post' Champion. Lost the title in her second year to one Grace Jones, an altogether less feminine creature with a hairstyle that looked as if she'd been hit on the head by a lift.

Pipe smoker of the Year.

All-England Yard-Of-Ale Champion. Never beaten. The beer was usually so frightened at the prospect of ending up all down her great hairy heaving chest, that it used to rush out of the glass with its hands up.

Played scrum-half for Hull Kingston Rovers rugby team for three and a half years. Banned for life for 'ungentlemanly behaviour' in the bath. Sadly missed by many as she was the only one who knew all 153 verses of 'Eskimo Nell'.

The only human to stay in a lift with Methane Minor for more than one floor.Apparently she can no longer smell a thing through her wrestler's nose, and the heady mixture of her after-shave, stale beer, tobacco, Chicken Kiev, armpits and jockstrap was so strong that Methane had to be carried out of the elevator unconscious on a stretcher.

TUESDAY APRIL 3RD

Hallo Dread Diary

Yes, me again. We're approaching the end of another term at Fishfriars Hall, which means the usual round of concerts, recitals and other events where we have a chance to embarass our parents. All these events are to be co-ordinated by our over-paid chinless Music Master, Mr Lloyd-Wobbler — or Old Cats' Eyes' as we know him, because he is so firmly fixed in the middle of the road.

Thursday afternoons were set aside for music lessons. Ours is what is known as a 'mixed-ability' class, which is a euphemistic way of saying that most of us are imbeciles.

At the very beginning of this week's lesson, Prince Luko, youngest member of the Royal Family, school half-wit and next in line for being photographed falling off horses, impressed Mr Lloyd-Wobbler by saying that he could read music, and with this he picked up a musical manuscript and demonstrated his skill. . . 'Tadpole, tadpole. . . circle, dot. . . squiggly thing, tadpole. . .' Mr Lloyd-Wobbler forced a patronising smile at the Royal untouchable and vented his frustrated anger by slamming Wimp Minor's head in the piano-lid. . .

The teacher's pet showed off by playing a solo on a row of trumpets. Sealions are such clever-dicks!

TUESDAY APRIL 3RD

Our odd-looking teacher decided to find out who were going to sing the solos for the School Easter Concert — his better-half, Sarah Brightspark, and Wimp Minor had a single in the charts anyway — an extract from 'Requiem to a Transport Cafe', entitled 'Pie and Cheese Roll', so they were naturally asked to perform that. Wimp Minor said he might have trouble getting those top notes every time, so Cowardly Major, our dormitory bully, offered his services with two trusty building-bricks, which not only guaranteed the high notes, but also offered the possibility of a harmony line if he trapped his thumbs between the bricks as well. . . Bygraves Major offered to perform his classic, 'Deck of Cards', but a survey of one hundred people suggested he go forth and multiply.

Auditions got underway. . . Sprinkler Peabody, the school bed-wetter, hopped up on the piano-stool and had a quick 'tinkle on the old ivories'.

Mr Lloyd-Wobbler watched in horror as the steam warped the lid of his favourite Steinway. . . 'You've ruined my grand piano! Now what am I going to play at the concert?' wailed our distraught teacher. . .'I've got a little-upright!' smirked Squinter Binns, reading a copy of 'Wobbly-Bits Weekly' by torchlight under his desk lid.

My personal contribution to the programme was to be to play 'The Trumpet Compulsory' — which is a bit like playing 'The Trumpet Voluntary', except they put an angry crocodile down your trousers if you refuse.

Dear little Punk Minimus did a very fair job of singing 'Oh For The Wings Of A Dove' as his solo piece, but Mr Lloyd-Wobbler suggested he keep the gobbing on the audience between stanzas down to a minimum.

Methane Minor was asked to perform his usual party-piece — reversing up to a flute and playing three choruses of the theme from 'Whistle Down The Wind', whilst drinking a glass of cabbage-water.

The soloists sorted out, Mr Lloyd-Wobbler decided to rehearse the school orchestra — Daley Maximus was on the fiddle, as usual. . . Dennis the Thorough Menace, Thatcher Major's Adonis-like sugar-daddy, had plenty of experience at playing second fiddle — and so the string section was formed. They lustily fiddled their way through the opening bars. . .

'Pizzicato! Pizzicato!' yelled their illustrious conductor. . . 'Nonsense! I haven't touched a drop all day!' lied Dennis, hiccoughing loudly and slumping forward, getting the prongs of his music-stand up his nose. . .

Baldy Kinnock, in charge of the wind and water section, came in carrying Wedgwood Bill and Benn Minor in a music case under his arm. . . 'What have you brought him for??' asked our unsightly teacher, 'I told you to bring your bassoon!'. . . 'Oh, sorry, Boyo!' growled Baldy, 'I thought you said "Bring a buffoon". . .'

Meanwhile poor dim-witted Prince Luko was trying to get a note out of the triangle he had been given to play. He passed out three times before Crawler Major, the school spoil-sport, told him that you don't blow a triangle, you hit it. 'Now, Your Highness,' said Mr Lloyd-Wobbler, almost bursting, purple with suppressed laughter. . . 'At the start of the piece, I want you and your triangle to open the bar. . .' 'Well when you do, mine's a double!' yelled Dennis, sliding off his chair and belching loudly.

All that remained was to get the Programmes for the night printed, which was something of a problem as the school had hit unforeseen financial difficulties — the school chaplain had embezzled £50,000 and run off with the Head Boy. . . however, Daley Minor reported that he knew a geezer what worked cheap, but we'd have to keep 'schtumm' as NALGO, this geezer's Union, poo-poos his operation and has black-listed him. After a quick call on the blower, a shifty-looking spiv with a John Bull Printing Outfit tucked under one arm, was spotted lurking around the school gate. . . So, of course, dear hopelessly mesmerised Diary, Mr Lloyd-Wobbler sidled up to Daley Minor and whispered. . . 'Pardon me boy, is that the chap that NALGO poo-poos?'. . .

Tonight as I lie back in my long-time-no-soapsuds sheets, I think: If Dennis the thorough Menace gets twenty pounds to go into town for the sheet music will he manage to get Beethoven, or will he just get Brahms and Liszt as usual.

FRIDAY APRIL 11TH

Hallo Dread Diary

Today was the end of the week once again — yes, Friday had crept round and was upon me once more — it's to be hoped Crusoe Minor never finds out, 'cause he gets ever so jealous!

This week was special though — it was Good Friday! . . . 'Yes, it was good for me too' mumbled Friday as he sneaked out of the back door.

We were due to disperse for the Easter Hols, but not 'til after the night's Easter Concert.

Dr Frotter, our highly-suspect Headmaster, said that he had found the perfect venue for the concert — the local equivalent of 'The Hollywood Bowl' — which turned out to be the local Maternity Clinic, 'The Pudding Bowl'.

The Fishfriars Hall Band opened the concert with a couple of bouncy numbers, but then they would be bouncy because, dear Diary, they were a Rubber Band!. . . The Conductor stood sullenly on his platform, refused to tell the band what tune to play next, paid everyone in hundredweight of pennies and head-butted Wimp Minor between the eyes and threw him out of the window because he couldn't find a seat — yes, you guessed it, he was a London Bus Conductor. . . The band really stretched themselves with their tricky final number. It was a good job they were an elastic band.

Then Mr Lloyd-Wobbler, our wealthy Music Teacher with the face like a Pekinese sucking a lemon, proudly announced that it was time for Sarah Brightspark, Placebo De Mango-Chutney and Wimp Minor to perform his latest money-spinning masterpiece, 'Requiem For A Strangled Tom-Cat'. . .

Rice Major immediately stood up and blew a huge raspberry — then he blew a huge Swiss Roll and a huge bowl of custard, covering poor Mr Lloyd-Wobbler, who appeared a trifle cross!. . .

Undeterred, the performance went on. . . and on. . . and on! There was a short interval after the first three or four hours to allow the audience to be revived with black coffee and oxygen-tents.

Poor little Wimp Minor collapsed through over-exertion. Somewhat surprisingly Cowardly Major, our dormitory bully, leapt to his rescue. 'Don't worry,' he said, 'I've heard that some musicians take "uppers" to keep them going during a long session'. . . and, with that, he ripped the soles off Wimp Minor's little patent leather buckle shoes and force-fed him the uppers, using a handy window-pole and his ever-trusty sink plunger.

Eventually it was the turn of the school orchestra, with their special guest conductor, ex-Head Boy, Heath Maximus — grinning some-time sailor and arch-opponent of teeth-capping. As he stood up, Thatcher Major put her tongue out at him and called him 'Wet'. He jeered back and called her a 'Rubber-faced rat-bag' — it was worrying to think that these ridiculously childish schoolkids might one day run the country.

FRIDAY APRIL 11TH

Mr Lloyd-Wobbler announced that Greig's Piano Concerto would have to be played on toilet paper and comb unless anyone could replace the school Grand Piano that Sprinkler Peabody, the school bed-wetter, had destroyed the previous week by having a quick tinkle on the ivories. . . 'I've got a gigantic rising Wurlitzer!' yelled Old Ben Flasher, the school caretaker, leaping up on stage and casually letting the straps of his denim boiler-suit slide sexily off his shoulders. . . to somewhere round his ankles.

Heath Maximus rapped his baton for silence. It didn't do much good — he'd wrapped it in pink paper with a huge ribbon and a large bow. . . Suddenly there was chaos! Nureyev Major accidentally over-tightened his already strained 'G-string', and gave an impromptu yodelling solo. . . Methane Minor saw the funny side of this and got another attack of the giggles, which caused the effect of his parents' Easter Tuck Parcel of hard-boiled Easter eggs, mushy peas and sprouts to manifest itself. . .

The resultant blast was so great and so intense that a voice yelled, 'We have lift-off ! ' — and Methane Minor soared upwards, crashing through 'The Pudding Bowl' roof and disappearing into the night sky, singing 'I'm A Rocket-Man' — and being monitored by a local radar-tracking station as a U.F.O. — and the 'F' certainly didn't stand for 'Flying'. . .

The next day when the Council Workmen came to repair the hole in the Pudding Bowl roof, they discovered that all the main beams and rafters had gone missing — Old Ben Flasher confessed to having burnt them on the school central-heating furnace. . .

or, as he actually put it, dear surprisingly-tolerant Diary. . . 'The roof of the Pudding is in the heating. . .'

In the small hours of the morning as I lie upon my louse-riddled lilo, I wonder whether Old Ben would ever go in search of the Lost Chord, or is he happier with his pyjama bottoms around his ankles. . .

Methane Minor in training for the 'World Freestyle Flatulance Championships'.

FISHFRIARS HALL SCHOOL REPORT

NAME	Methane Minor (Fifth Form)		
SUBJECT	ACHIEVEMENT	EFFORT	REMARKS
MATHS	F-	F-	He's a little stinker!
ENGLISH	F-	F-	His end of term essay about his exploits in the dormitory, entitled 'Wind in the Pillows', was in very poor taste.
GEOGRAPHY			
BIOLOGY ENVIRONMENTAL STUDIES			
LATIN ~~FRENCH~~			"FLATULUS ASPHYXO CLAUSTROPHOBIA" (WHICH ROUGHLY MEANS HE IS BANNED FROM MY CLASSROO
HISTORY	F-	F-	Has a morbid facination with gas attacks of the First World War.
SCIENCE			Very enthusiastic when it comes to the synthesis of toxic gases.

TERM SPRING

SUBJECT	ACHIEVEMENT	EFFORT	REMARKS
ART HANDICRAFTS			
GAMES PHYSICAL EDUCATION	A+	A+	VERY GOOD AT BOXING. FIGHTS UNDER THE SEMI-PRO NAME OF 'GASEOUS CLAY' – A KNOCKOUT EVERY TIME!
~~RELIGIOUS INSTRUCTION~~ MUSIC	F–	F–	VERY ACTIVE IN the Wind Section

GENERAL PROGRESS:

Has a serious personality problem. Nobody seems to be able to get close to him.

(Please stop sending him hard-boiled eggs and sprouts in his tuck parcels.)

ATTENDANCE Far too often for everyone's liking.

FORM TEACHER'S SIGNATURE Mr Hat-Trick

HEAD TEACHER'S SIGNATURE Dr Frotter

PARENT'S SIGNATURE LORD METHANE OF WINDRUSH

TUESDAY APRIL 15TH

Well what a business Dire Dreary

It was supposed to be Easter Hols at Fishfriars Hall — a time for relaxation; for sitting in traffic jams on the M25; a time for blaming the Russians for the torrential rain when you get the picnic-basket out; and a time for eating chocolate eggs, until such time as one has had an adequate sufficiency — last year I knew exactly when I had eaten enough Easter Eggs — I was sick on the cat!

This year, however, hols were not to be quite the same. . . We had all volunteered to take part in a Foreign-Exchange scheme — I say volunteered — in fact we weren't going to volunteer until we saw what happened when Chancer Minimus told Mr Don Corleoni, the Italian master and school Godfather, that he didn't want to take part, and woke up the next morning to find a head in bed with him — no, not the head of a horse — much worse! The Head of a nearby all-boys' Choral College, Dr Nine-Bob-Note, who was blowing in his ear and fluttering his eyelashes. . .

Our parents seemed enthusiastic about this Foreign Exchange — in fact my own dear Pater asked if he could swop me for a blonde Swedish air-hostess and a packet of Venezuelan stamps. . .

We thankfully were given a choice of exchange destinations, as our own 'Twin-Town', due either to an almighty clerical clanger or a huge back-hander, was Barnsley. . .

Methane Minor, the ever-flatulent fifth former, marathon mushy-peas eating champion and holder of the world record for emptying a packed tube train during rush-hour, said that he was going to 'The Windy City'. 'Oh,' I said, 'Chicago?'. . . 'No,' he replied, 'Brussels!' — referring I think to a peculiar side-effect of his favourite food, sprouts. . .

Of course, the most popular place for the Exchange, as always, was France. Bunter Major, the disgusting fat pig of the Lower Remove, was getting into the French mood, and had taken to chasing Aznavour Minor round the Quadrangle with a knife and fork and a mincing-machine, ever since he'd heard that you can eat frogs' legs.

Sprinkler Peabody, the school bed-wetter, was to stay with a French farmer and his family. The ever-steaming little fellow drank 27 pints of cold lager, a crate of orange juice and five buckets of water on the non-stop coach to the farm-house — during which time he ruined the entire party's footwear and invalidated the coach company's underseal anti-rust guarantee.

The farmer very wisely insisted Sprinkler sleep out in the barn — unfortunately the sound of the rain on the roof made him responsible for spoiling the whole year's corn harvest and drowning three sheep. . . Sprinkler suggested that the farmer could still get rid of the corn, making a selling-point of the fact that it was *young*, slightly-immature corn — in other words, it was just a little wet behind the ears. . .

The French have a somewhat limited sense of fun

at the best of times, and this gentleman was no exception — he put poor Sprinkler through the combine-harvester, all the time screaming French obscenities about English lamb being like eating stewed raincoats, and Englishmen making love with their bowler-heads on — whatever all that meant.

Some of the chaps were staying with Paris boys, some were staying with Avignon boys, but Gender-Bender Major seemed extremely keen to stay with a boy from Nancy. . .

Old Ben Flasher, the school caretaker, volunteered to supervise the party destined for St Tropez, where he had read that you can let it all hang out. His eagerness to indulge in a Naturist-type holiday was so great that he had his trousers down round his ankles by the time they got to the Terminal Gate at Heathrow.

Cowardly Major, our dormitory bully, had been banned from travelling to Europe, after his last trip when he smashed up half of Paris. Ordinarily he would have been given 15 years in prison, but fortunately he had the good sense to disguise himself as a football fan, so that the British Embassy would put it down to youthful high spirits and let him off with a caution. . . He therefore asked Wimp Minor to do some smuggling for him. It was difficult for the poor little Wimp to say 'No', when Cowardly Major had a firm grip on his tonsils with a pair of pliers and was threatening him with photographs of Russell Harty and Bonny Langford at close range. . .

The poor little chap struggled manfully all the way home from France with a huge heavy crate for the bully. The crunch came when Cowardly Major approached to check his smuggled haul — it was the crunch of skull meeting skull. Sensing trouble and realising Wimp Minor's grave error, I made a hasty retreat.

As I turned to run, I saw the irate bully using a Parisian umbrella and his ever-trusty sink plunger to force-feed Wimp Minor the huge crate, its contents and a dozen French loaves — sideways! Apparently Cowardly Major's short fuse had blown when Wimp Minor casually said, 'I don't know what you want two gross of French Lettuce for anyway — you haven't even got a rabbit. . .'

As I disappeared I heard screams and the awful buzz of a chainsaw, as Cowardly Major callously amputated all of Wimp Minor's limbs. Apparently, Tex Fritter, our School Chef, never one to waste anything, picked up the severed limbs, minced them and used them to make a famous Greek dish, which appeared on the menu next day dear ever-gullible Diary as. . . 'Tex's Chainsaw Moussaka. . .'

And so, alone upon my manky moth-eaten mattress I muse on Methane Minor and his Duty-Free booze: If he spent the night drinking Bells, would he be dropping clangers all the next day? . . .

MONDAY APRIL 28TH

Well Dead Dreary

Another day, another dollar. Today was the first day of a new term at Fishfriars Hall — the school becoming increasingly famous for preparing boys, who are too rich and far too stupid to ever get jobs, for the difficult life ahead of them. The prefects study for 'A' levels in 'Talking loudly in restaurants'; 'Getting drunk and driving Porsches into bus queues'; and 'The various ways of torturing little furry animals to death, whilst perched on a horse'. . .

Nobody likes going back to school after the hols, but some had to be dragged bodily through the school gates, screaming — there was the Headmaster, Matron, and quite a few of the teachers.

Cowardly Major, our dormitory bully, was the first to come through the great iron school gates. He gave me a cheery knee in the groin for old time's sake and then dropped the nut on my pet hamster. . .

Then Wimp Minor came rushing down the drive with his trouser seat on fire and leapt into the school duck pond. . . Sparky Butane, the school arsonist, followed him, smiling knowlingly to himself, and trying to conceal a flame-thrower down the leg of his shorts. . .

Squinter Binns was the next to arrive, carrying a satchel full of magazines, like 'Kiss My Whip' and

'Wobbly Bits Weekly'. He peered at me blindly through his thick glasses and shook me by the hand with one of his increasingly hairy palms.

Suddenly there was quite a commotion — a taxi drew up with all its windows open. The driver was coughing, spluttering and looking quite ill. He screeched his cab to a halt and hurled out his apparently antisocial passengers, Methane Minor, the flatulent fifth former, and his pungent parent, Lord Methane of Windrush, on to the gravel drive. Apparently he blamed them for the death of his cab mascot and pet canary, Norman, which was laid spark out at the bottom of its cage. . . yes dear despairing Diary, it was an ill wind that blew Norman no good!. . .

Lord Methane gave Methane Minor a tuck parcel of sprouts, hard-boiled eggs, baked beans, Guinness and marrowfat peas, and a moment later was gone with the wind. . .

Prince Luko, youngest member of the Royal Family, was, as usual, keen to arrive back at school with the minimum of fuss, so that he would not be treated any differently to the other boys. . . A relatively small platoon of buglers heralded the arrival of the Royal Helicopter with an unpretentious 10 minute fanfare. Prince Luko was then winched down from the helicopter in a golden throne, with a scantily-clad girl sitting on each knee. They were his latest Swedish girlfriends, Koosheez and Lika — Koosheez Starkers and Lika Rabbett — apparently they had been appointed as our new School Dinner ladies and were carrying quite vicious looking canes.

When everyone had arrived, the Headmaster, Dr

Frotter, sent a message round the school with a British dwarf and an African pygmy — yes, dear tortured Diary, they were a couple of 24 inch, black and white monitors.

The message was that we were all to assemble in the Main Hall so that the Head could address us. . . All the jokers who turned up wearing stamped luggage labels were immediately publicly garotted with piano wire.

The awesome Headmaster banged his hand for silence. He screamed in pain, because he had banged it with a rather large mallet! Dr Frotter gave the impression of distinct displeasure, then he gave his impressions of Frank Carson and Groucho Marx, then he finished his opening spot roller-skating on one leg and playing 'My Way' on the spoons.

The Arch-Beako concluded the morning assembly by instructing us all to visit a local chap, Andrew Robbin, who makes the best cricket bats money can buy, to buy ourselves a bat for the forthcoming season. He warned us, however, that Andy was a bit of a rough-diamond — rather vulgar, always swearing and, getting his only pleasure from sailing single-handed round The Cape every year. I will never forget the Head's final reminder to us as long as I live, and I'm sure you won't either, dear diving-for cover Diary. His actual words were: 'Don't forget boys — first thing in the morning, go and see. . . bat-man Andy Robbin, the Cape crude sailor. . .'

MONDAY APRIL 28TH

As I lounge around on my biologically-stained bedspread, I muse to myself — if Methane Minor gets caught again this term raiding the kitchen for mushy peas, baked beans and sprouts — will he leave Fishfriars Hall under a cloud??

The villagers looking singularly unconvinced as Thatcher Major tries to explain that Dennis-The-Thorough-Menace is suffering from sunstroke in the middle of January.

WEDNESDAY MAY 7TH

Dear Diary

Settling down after Easter and Spring was in the air — Wimp Minor's Jack-in-the-box had gone berserk!. . . The lid was also in the air, and the little rubber clown had shot out of the Dormitory window!. . . I think it may have had something to do with the fact that Cowardly Major, our dormitory bully, had been giving the Jack-in-the-box a 12,000 Doinngg! service with his trusty sledgehammer. . .

Fishfriars Hall looked lovely at this time of the year — the early blooms were beginning to show. The school garden was a blaze of yellow and blue — someone had set fire to a Chinese Policeman!

Unfortunately, the vast crop of bulbs had all failed to grow this year — which was probably because ex-London cabby Fred Goosegog, the school gardener, after a hearty meal of home-grown magic mushroom omelette, had planted 5 gross of 40 watt electric light bulbs. . .

Fred had also pruned the school roses. . . Cowardly Major had similarly 'pruned' Wimp Minor — 'Pruning' in this case being the traditional Fishfriars torture whereby a bully force-feeds a smaller chap with a hudredweight of canteen prunes, and then nails all the lavatory doors up!

We younger fellows are always co-opted to help out

in the garden at this time of year. I say 'co-opted' — that's actually a euphemistic way of saying that the Headmaster threatened the entire school with a cruel punishment — a visit from Lord Longford — if we refused. . .

Russian-Athlete Major as usual, refused to take part, so the Head summoned him to his Study after Prayers and took out his special broken-glass-encrusted cane. . . 'This is going to hurt me more than it hurts you, boy!' the Arch-Beako sighed and began viciously flogging himself and sceaming in ecstasy!

Old Ben Flasher, the school caretaker, was sitting in a corner of the garden, his trousers down round his ankles, spraying his gooseberries!. . . They looked ridiculous purple!. . . He was also helping the gardener to tend his prize chrysanmythums. . . crithasanmy. . . crimeanthisums — Roses! — in order that they could show them at the Annual Village Show. Old Ben Flasher, of course, already had a name locally for showing his rhubarb!. . . I understand the name most commonly used was 'dirty old degenerate'!

Sprinkler Peabody, the school bed-wetter, was given an appropriate task — watering the school lawn. The incontinent little chap tackled the task in his own peculiar style — he drank 5 crates of ice-cold Cola, and the contents of the greenhouse rain-butt and then listened to a cassette of Niagara Falls on his 'Walkman', while hurtling round on the school merry-go-round. . .

It was soon time to sort out the bedding-plants. Gender-Bender Major eagerly volunteered to weed out the pansies. . . He was an expert in flower-beds —

mind you he claimed to be better than most in candy-striped sleeping bags as well. Gender-Bender Major also volunteered to touch up the borders — which came as a great relief to the 'day-boys'. . .

All the delicate and exotic bedding-plants had to be put in a sheltered place. 'What we need is a wind-break' said Mr Goosegog, leading with his chin. . . Methane Minor, the ever-flatulent fifth former's eyes lit up. . .

'I'm an expert wind-breaker sir!' he chirped up, giving an earth-scorching demonstration which registered 35 on the Richter Scale, broke every window in the school greenhouse and suffocated the caretaker's dog. . .

As a result Methane Minor was made school scarecrow, keeping the birds off the newly-planted seeds — the poor asphyxiated creatures plummetting like stones from the polluted sky above him. . .

Meanwhile, the rest of us had been instructed to clean out the school duck-pond. First we needed to drain the dirty water out. Cowardly Major had a brainwave — he pushed Bunter Major, the disgusting fat pig of the Lower Remove, face down in the mud next to the pond and then shoved a couple of chipolata sausages down the fat buffoon's voluminous, tent-like shorts, followed closely by the ever-hungry school ferret. The huge shorts billowed and thrashed as the sounds of chomping teeth were heard.

Eventually the inevitable happened and, just as Bunter Major went cross-eyed with pain, and began sucking in a huge agonised gulp of air, Cowardly Major shoved his head into the pond and miraculously the putrid festering water disappeared. . . Squinter Binns was delighted by the results, for there, at the bottom of the drained pond was a horde of French dirty books which had been dumped there by the school's 'Vice' Captain during a police raid — yes, as if you hadn't got there for yourself hours ago dear amazingly-patient Diary, we'd found a load of. . . 'Frogs' porn. . .'

Prostrate upon my preposterously pungent pillow, I think about Bunter Major, my porky pal. If he'd really drunk all that dirty pond water, should he go on the Pill to prevent himself from becoming stagnant? . . .

The three women who are kept permanently employed to do Sprinkler Peabody's laundry.

SATURDAY MAY 10TH

Dear Diary

I was woken up this morning by the sound of torrential rain, which was lashing against the crumbling stone walls of Fishfriars Hall.

Tropical countries have their 'Rainy Seasons' — We have a similar thing — we call it 'the Cricket Season'. . . And so it was, with our hearts in our mouths, that we were ordered out to the freezing cricket pavilion. . .

We had our hearts in our mouths because we had been playing an illicit game of Poker and had almost been caught by the duty prefect, Bronter Major. Bygraves Minor, the school fat-head, had a brainwave to get rid of the incriminating 'Deck of Cards'. The hearts he popped into our mouths. . . the clubs reminded him of stone-age man, so we burnt them before Bronter saw us. . . the spades reminded him of buckets and spades at the seaside, so we sold them for a ridiculous profit, and of course the moment they were sold, they disintegrated. . . the diamonds reminded him of a girl's best friend, so we pushed them down the front of Nureyev Major's tights. . .

It's a pity we were interrupted as we had only just decided on a game of Poker. Wimp Minor wanted to play 'Happy Families'. . . Gender-Bender Major wanted to play 'Strip Jack Naked' — you should have seen Jack run!. . .

SATURDAY MAY 10TH

Methane Minor was something of a past master at 'Trumps'. . . and Cowardly Major, our dormitory bully, grabbed hold of Wimp Minor's pale skinny little leg and wanted to play 'Snap'. Wimp Minor said he couldn't play Poker as he didn't know what a Royal Flush was. . . Cowardly Major could hardly believe his luck! He quickly dragged the shrieking little chap to Prince Luko's private loo, popped his head in the basin and pulled the chain. . .

Prince Luko is an ideal opponent for Poker, because you can always tell when he has got a good hand — every time he picks up a King or a Queen, he shouts out 'Pater!' or 'Mater!'. . . But I digress. . .

Back to the cricket pavilion! Mr Hitler, our ever-compassionate Games Master, was jovially castrating a boy with a length of rusty cheese wire for forgetting his cricket togs. . .

Prince Luko had heard that we were expected to wear a pair of flannels. The poor dim-witted chap caused the elderly secretary, Miss Virgo-Intacta, to clutch for her smelling-salts when he emerged wearing only two face-cloths — a knotted one on his head and the other round his wrist for a sweat-band. The rest of use were properly dressed in our cricket kit — and had been fitted with a groin-protecting 'box' — all except the well-blessed Nureyev Major that is, who had been fitted with a 'packing case'.

Mr Hitler asked somebody to fetch a set of stumps — so Cowardly Major gleefully started his trusty chainsaw and began hacking the limbs off First Formers. 'We also need a couple of cricket balls!' yelled Mr Hitler. . . Fortunately Mr Frankenstein, the

SATURDAY MAY 10TH

Biology Master, overheard this dangerous request and hastily hid the school crickets. . .

Mr Hitler concentrated first on bowling. He demonstrated the curious art of polishing the ball against the front of one's trousers. . . Squinter Binns, the stunted little wreck, spent the next 2½ ecstatic

DR FROTTE
SOME CLASSI

The cut through silly point

The slice through covers

hours practising nothing else!. . . We believe this is the first recorded case of anyone falling passionately in love with a cricket ball — Sadly it was doomed not to work — Claire Rayner told the devastated chap that you should never get too involved with a partner who'd been caught on the rebound.

DEMONSTRATES STROKES

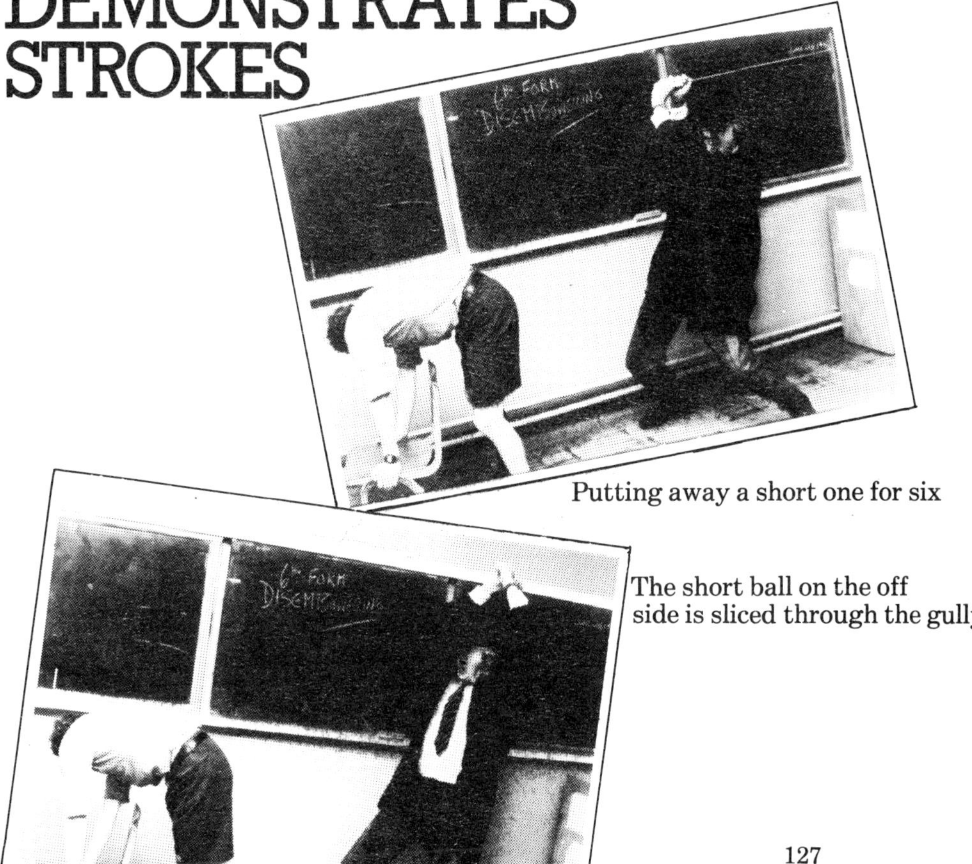

Putting away a short one for six

The short ball on the off side is sliced through the gully

SATURDAY MAY 10TH

Half the boys were sent out to field. . . Gender-Bender Major always fielded in slips — usually with silk stockings and matching undies. . . Glitter Major was 'square-leg' — which was emphasised by his 'square' trousers — flared lamé hipsters — and ridiculously dated silver platform boots. . .

Dennis-The-Thorough-Menace, Thatcher Major's bronzed sugar-daddy and school falling down and hiccupping champion, staggered out of the changing-rooms with a couple of his drinking chums. He was our extremely Silly Mid-Off — his chums being a very giggly wicket-keeper and a totally paralytic Short-Leg, who kept tripping over his long trousers. . .

The rest of us were to bat against this awe-inspiring side. . . Boycott Minimus wasn't allowed to go in first, so he sulked and took his bat home. . . Eventually a replacement bat was found — all covered in blood and hair. . . No, not as you might think, dear too-clever-by-half Diary, it wasn't a Vampire Bat! It was the one which the Headmaster used to cuff the Juniors about the head.

The first chap, Saville Maximus, winner of the school booby-prize for public-speaking, went in to bat. The opposing Captain donned a black business-man's hat with evil horns sticking out of the top of it — yes, dear less-sure-of-yourself-now Diary, he'd put on his 'Demon Bowler'. . .

Saville Maximus started trembling to such an extent that the sound of the rattling of his jewellery was mistaken for a passing Hare Krishna band. . . Cowardly Major paced out his 4-mile run-up to bowl, hurtled towards the crease and delivered a perfect leg-break — his next ball was higher and this time broke

Saville Maximus's nose as well and knocked all his teeth out. . .

Cowardly Major appealed to Mr Hitler, the Umpire — you could tell that because the master kept blowing kisses to the bully. 'Owzat! Face before wicket!!' shrieked Cowardly Major. . . Saville Maximus was carried off the pitch spitting teeth and mumbling incoherently — but then he always does. . . 'Now then, as it happens! Howzat then? A face full of leather and cork for Uncle Jimmy!'

The next chap in was Slogger Harris who got a 'Duck' — the poor thing didn't half quack as it fell to the ground like a stone.

By the time Cowardly Major had maimed half a dozen of our team for life, the rest of us lost our nerve, ripped off our cricket togs and hurled them into the air, along with our cricket bats, to shower down on the fielding team as we fled in the opposite direction. Yes, I suppose you could say, dear disbelieving Diary, it was. . . 'raining bats and togs.'

Tonight as I lie thinking about the match and scratching in my barbarous holiday-home for bed-bugs, I wonder why when Methane Minor was at the wicket did the bails keep flying off before the ball had even left the Bowler's hand. . .?

SUNDAY MAY 25TH

Dear Diary

Here we are again. It was morning assembly at Fishfriars Hall. The Headmaster, Dr Frotter, was giving his usual address — 13 Tight-Gusset Crescent — which, by a strange coincidence, we'd seen in a 'Contact' magazine as the address of a strange chap called 'Naughty Norman', who apparently needed strict discipline from a nanny in rubber.

The tedious Arch-Beako's voice was very nearly drowned by the sounds of snoring. You would have thought the rest of the staff would have tried to stay awake! As I looked round at my chums, it was obvious that they weren't paying much attention either. Cowardly Major, our dormitory bully, was absent-mindedly disembowelling a couple of first formers with a specially customised hover-mower.

Prince Luko was having the Arch-Beako's speech translated into words of one syllable by his minder, food-taster, Page Three girl-sampler and Gorillagram deliverer — no costume necessary.

Collins Major, the Extremely Senior Girl and school 'Horizontal-Mixed-Wrestling' Champion, was idly twisting the tourniquet in the middle of her back, to take up the day's slack in her skin. I remember, as her face stretched like an African drum and her smile broadened for the thousandth time, wondering how far past her ears her smile will go before the top of her head falls off.

Squinter Binns, the self-abused little wreck, was intently studying his hymn book and huskily singing to himself, 'All Things Bare And Beautiful'. Closer inspection revealed that his hairy, trembling little palms were holding the latest issue of 'Wobbly Bits Weekly' inside the battered hymn book. . .

Meanwhile Dr Frotter was giving out the school notices — I was lucky, I got two — a lovely wooden one which read 'Keep Off The Grass', and a hand-drawn one which said, 'No Sniggering During Sex Education Classes — Maximum Penalty, public stoning!' Incidentally, Dennis The Thorough Menace, Thatcher Major's iron-pumping hulk and freelance village idiot, was publicly stoned last week on the village green — when he got back to school he was sobered up and given a severe thrashing. . .

The Arch-Beako rounded off by telling us that we were all to enjoy a day by the river as it was a Bank Holiday weekend. And so we all looked forward to a warm sunny Sunday. All except Fatty Bunter, the disgusting fat pig of the Lower Remove, that is, who said he was looking forward to an extra-large strawberry sundae with crushed nuts. The best we could do was to handcuff him to Methane Minor, the ever-flatulent fifth former, which promised him a Sunday full of ripe raspberries, and Cowardly Major, with his ever-trusty meat tenderising mallet, was more than happy to oblige the obese young chap with the crushed nuts.

Being a Sunday we all put on our best clothes. As we

walked to the river, a vision of loveliness appeared on the horizon, in a stunning see-through white lace dress, broad-brimmed white hat and white sandals — He's an odd sort of a chap, but you can't deny Gender-Bender Major has good taste. . . Nevertheless the Headmaster was furious and boxed the sexually-confused young fellow about the ears with a 10-foot barge pole — Personally, I wouldn't have gone near him with one in that outfit. . . 'I've never been so embarassed in my life!' yelled Dr Frotter. . . 'Sorry sir,' sobbed Gender-Bender Major, 'How was I supposed to know you'd be wearing the same dress??'

The girls also looked quite lovely standing by the water's edge. Parton Maximus appeared to be sensibly wearing a very well inflated life-jacket under her blouse.

Lauper Minor, the shy retiring American girl with the voice like a cracked train whistle, had her natural-looking green and orange locks in a particularly silly 'Peek-A-Boo' hairdo and Old Ben Flasher, the school caretaker, was wearing a 'Peek-A-Boo' boiler-suit — I'm not quite sure which was the most horrific — the sight revealed by Old Ben's cut-away dungarees, or the sight revealed when Lauper Minor's hair parted to show her huge red slash of a mouth, looking like the result of the shower attack in 'Psycho'.

Parton Maximus stood alone, looking for all the world like an Alpine over-hang, fluttering her huge eyelashes at a passing bus load of navvies. Unfortunately, due to the excessive movements, the eyelashes fluttered right into the river. As she somewhat inelegantly hitched her skirt up, knelt down in the mud and leaned over the bank to fish them out, the forces of gravity took over, and in she went!. . .

How we laughed as she tried desperately to swim on her front, but her natural buoyancy kept making her bob upside down onto her back.

Lichfield Minor took a snapshot of this amusing phenomenon, which has since been mistaken by experts to be a perfect photo of the twin humps of the Loch Ness Monster.

Meanwhile, Collins Major was languishing seductively on the bank, when suddenly, for no apparent reason, she slapped her ice cream cornet on the end of her nose. This sort of thing happens fairly frequently to her, as every time she has her face lifted, her mouth changes position and can prove quite tricky to find. Some people think she suffers from bad acne — in fact the spots are scars where she's been stabbing away with a fork full of bangers and mash, desperately searching for the new position of her erstwhile cake-hole. . . She'd recently had the same problem in an exclusive Chinese restaurant where their speciality is a pancake filled with hickory-smoked duckling and chicory tips, which she pushed into the middle of her over-stretched clock where her mouth had once been. She apologised to the waiter for the wastage — her actual words in fact, dear devastated Diary, were. . . 'Sorry about the. . . Hickory Chickory Duck, but my mouth's run up my clock. . .'

SUNDAY MAY 25TH

As I lie tonight snugly wrapped up in my putrefying pyjamas I ponder: If Methane Minor stood on a Duck Board and suddenly lost his self control, would he windsurf himself out to sea?. . .

MONDAY MAY 26TH

Hallo Dread Diary

You may remember yesterday I was telling you about the Fishfriars Hall Bank Holiday Sunday by the river.

We had all put on our Sunday best. Wimp Minor was wearing a bright blazer — Cowardly Major, our dormitory bully, had set his duffel coat on fire!. . . Methane Minor was wearing bell-bottomed trosers — which was very confusing, because everyone kept thinking they could hear a phone ringing. . .

Dennis The Thorough Menace, Thatcher Major's minder and founder of the 'Chinless Is Beautiful' movement, had settled on a pair of see-through shorts — vodka and gin. . .

The afternoon by the river was the brainchild of Dr Frotter, our 'oddball' Headmaster as Matron calls him (apparently Adolf Hitler had the same problem. . .) He proudly announced it was time for us to get out on to the water. He untied a rowing-boat and said, 'All I need is a couple of oars, and I'm set'. . . Only the laws of libel prevent me from telling you dear Diary which two girls volunteered. . .

Dr Frotter was horrified! He turned to his Deputy Head, Mr Stringweed, and said, 'See to those two naughty girls for me!'. . . 'What?? Both of them?? I've had a bad back!' pleaded Stringweed. . . 'No! Punish

Collins Major, the extremely senior girl, demonstrating her new virtually-invisible face stretching device.

them you fool!'. . . As the girls miserably followed the deputy Head back to the school, Dr Frotter silenced our cheers and continued. . .

'Right, does anyone require any instructions on rowing?' 'I could do with a few wrinkles' said Collins Major, the extremely Senior Girl. . . 'Good grief!' murmured Krystle Minor, the school chiropodist's nightmare, 'You've already got more wrinkles than the EEC Prune Mountain. . .' On hearing this, Collins Major leapt on Krystle Minor, and the two of them wrestled in the mud for several minutes. As they were dragged apart, Dr Frotter spotted our somewhat drained Deputy Head crawling back from the direction of Fishfriars Hall. . .

'Ah, Stringweed! Just in time! Two more miscreants for you to deal with! — How did you go on with the other two?'. . . 'They won't be able to sit down for a day or so, Headmaster. . .' Apparently the emaciated little chap had gloss-painted their school chairs. . .

Eventually the Arch-Beako returned to his rowing-lesson. He told us that the best oars for ease of sculling down the river were slim-bladed, light-weight ones. . . Cowardly Major begged to differ and said heavy, broad hardwood oars were the best for skulling, and proved it by clouting Wimp Minor over the head with one. . .

'Now' said the Head, 'What is this thing called at the back of the boat, that you pull from side to side to steer?'. . .

'The Hun sir! The Hun!!' yelled Tarbuck Major, the school clever-dick. . . And I'm sure you can imagine what he said next, dear dumbfounded Diary. . . 'It must be The Hun — because it's. . . a tiller! Boom-boom!'

With Tarbuck Major duly thrown into the drink, the Head continued. . . Unfortunately Tarbuck Major was laughing so much at his own joke that he ruined the drink, and poor old Dennis The Thorough Menace shot himself — fortunately the bullet passed through a part of the body where it would do him no permanent harm — it went right through his head. . .

The Arch-Beako went on, 'Now when you're steering the boat, we talk about Port and Starboard. Does anybody know which side Port is on?'

'A bit on the sweet side old thing!' hiccoughed Dennis The Thorough Menace, 'But a damned sight better than nothing when the brandy runs out,' and with that he fell face down in the mud again.

We were only allowed to row up the river as far as the marker buoy — the boy in question was none other than Wimp Minor with a huge boulder tied to his ankle.

One thing I didn't understand — on the seats of all the boats, there were carvings which read. . . 'Tina's tummy-button, nine out of ten. . . Suzanne's tummy-button, ten out of ten. . .' and so on. . . I could only assume, dear never-had-it-so-bad Diary, that they were. . . 'Naval Ratings'. . . With jokes like that around, it was a merciful release when night fell. . .

Dennis The Thorough Menace also fell for the hundredth time. . . but the day wasn't over — The Arch-Beako had erected a marquee in one corner of the field — apparently it was the only marquee in the world to be made of studded leather and manacle chains — Yes, dear wondering-where-it-will-all-end Diary, it was the Marquee de Sade!

Dr Frotter prided himself in keeping up with the times and had signed a top rock band for us to dance to — 'Ernest Hardisty And His Hit Parade Combo' — Cowardly Major certainly seemed to enjoy them — headbanging the night away. . . Other people's heads of course — he was banging them into tables, wooden posts, beer bottles. . . The Combo were playing heavy metal numbers, like 'The Birdie Song', and a medley of the Smurfs Golden Greats. . . Cowardly Major slicked back his hair and approached a gorgeous girl and growled, 'Are you dancing?' The girl gave the usual answer, 'Are you asking?' 'Are you stupid or what?? I've just asked, haven't I??!!' the bully yelled, and he

From the Office of
The Headmaster

FISHFRIARS HALL

Dear Matron

Thank you for the komplimentury tikket to come and wotch you in akshum. I havent bean to a good old - fashuned mud-Wrestling match for years.

Perhaps we could meat up after the fight for a few pints of Best Bitter and share a pipe of baccy together.

Then back to your place for a good game of "Trying to give A specimen" just like the old days.

yours as orlways

coochie snuggles.

nutted her between the eyes. . .

Squinter Binns, the hairy-palmed pervert, was hanging round a group of young dancing debutantes, with his hands plunged deep into his shabby gaberdine pockets. . . He'd heard something about debutantes 'coming-out' at dances, and if one was going to come out tonight, he wasn't going to miss it. . .

I was keeping well clear of the dance floor as I seemed to have been born with two left feet — which has one advantage — I'm one of the few people who can go shop-lifting for shoes.

Suddenly I was aware of a strange blonde girl trying to attract my attention — she was hitting me over the head with her handbag and kneeing me in the groin. . . It was Ewing Minimus, a stunted little thing who apparently had been hit on the head by a lift when she was a child. . .

I was ever so embarassed as she sat herself opposite me, giving me the eye — I quickly polished it for her and gave it back. . . 'Why don't you take me back to your dormitory?' she whispered. 'No fear!' I said, 'I don't want to go to bed yet, I'm staying here to enjoy myself!'

She was not easily deterred. Huskily she whispered, 'Have you ever had sexual relations?'. . . 'Well, I had an Aunty who got around a bit' I volunteered.

'Listen!' she said, smashing a bottle over my head, 'I've got a Vauxhall Viva parked outside. It's got a puncture, but if you change the wheel for me, I'll let you take me down Lovers' Lane.'

'But just a minute!' I said, panicking, 'If I change your wheel I'll probably get an incriminating funny grease stain on my shirt'. . . 'Not if you use the special spanner in the boot!' she insisted. . . At that moment Ernest Hardisty's Hit Parade Combo struck up a classic Spanish flamenco tune, and Ewing Minimus sang these words, dear daily disintegrating Diary. . . 'If you want to avoid the funny stain, Bring my Viva wheel-spanner. . .'

Later, lying snug in my rat-infested romper suit, I wonder if anyone was silly enough to go down Lovers' Lane with Ewing Minimus. Just how does one neck with a girl who hasn't got one?

FISHFRIARS HALL SCHOOL REPORT

NAME	Collins Major (Extremely Senior Girl)		
SUBJECT	ACHIEVE-MENT	EFFORT	REMARKS
MATHS	A+	A+	Very good with big numbers. (Coach parties catered for by prior arrangement.)
ENGLISH	F-	F-	I don't know what all the fuss is about
DRAMA ~~GEOGRAPHY~~	F–	F–	NOR DO I! (IN ANYCASE, SHE CAN'T ACT + FINDS IT IMPOSSIBLE TO DISPLAY HUMAN EMOTIONS – PREHAPS SHE SHOULD GET INTO TV SOAP OPERAS)
BIOLOGY ENVIRONMENTAL STUDIES	A+	A+	Excellent in the field. (and not half bad in the greenhouse) - Mr Gooseggog
FRENCH	69	100	Mon dieu!
HISTORY	A+	A+	She's lived through a good deal of it.
SCIENCE			A most obliging girl (I wish she was in my dormitory).

TERM SUMMER

SUBJECT	ACHIEVEMENT	EFFORT	REMARKS
ART HANDICRAFTS	A+	A1	A shining example of what is possible with a needle and thread.
GAMES PHYSICAL EDUCATION	A+	A+	HER 20 MINUTE ROUTINE ON THE MAT IS BREATH-TAKING. (SHE CAN WORK UP A SWEAT OVER THE VAULTING HORSE TOO – MR HITLER)
~~RELIGIOUS INSTRUCTION~~ CREATIVE STUDIES	A+	A+	VERY GOOD WITH POLYFILLA AND A TROWEL.

GENERAL PROGRESS:

Extremely popular with most of the masters (and the local army base). Very accommodating.

ATTENDANCE Confined to bed a good deal of the time but ~~doesn't let this hamper~~ her education.

FORM TEACHER'S SIGNATURE Miss Brick Out-House

HEAD TEACHER'S SIGNATURE Dr Frotter

PARENT'S SIGNATURE Mrs Collins (The somewhat dithery hand of a 110 year old woman)

WEDNESDAY JUNE 25TH

Dear Diary

Today was a very special day at Fishfriars. I walked with a spring in my heel — my watch had exploded. . . so I was also walking with a second-hand up my nose and a winder in my tummy-button. . . I made a mental note to give my watch-mender a ticking-off.

I passed Jennings in the corridor, and rather wished I'd never eaten him in the first place.

As I walked further along the oak-panelled hall I looked up at the busts of previous headmasters — I'd seen them all before over the years on Page Three of The Sun.

Just then, I saw a familiar sight at Fishfriars — a boy wrapped in white paper with his hair on fire. . . yes, dear Diary, he was a 'fag'.

The reason for my excitement was that today was the school Sports Day.

It's a day which typifies the fine ideals of the British education system — glory for the big-heads and show-offs. . . and public humiliation for under-achievers and the over-weight.

The groundsman had come out of hibernation and broken into a snail's-pace. He'd cut the grass on the playing-fields — something which he did every year, whether it needed it or not.

The Headmaster had been down to the Pawn Shop to

Gender-Bender Major waving to the trainer, in the fond hope he'll run on and give him a rub down with a wet sponge.

get the trophies out of hock for the day. . . and Mr Hitler, the Games Master, had devised a new track event called 'The Hand Grenade And Spoon Race', which he felt would keep us on our toes. . . in fact, very few of us now have toes.

Our Housemaster, Mr Hat-trick, (although we all nicknamed him Jerry) was posted to the school gates to welcome the parents. . . Unfortunately, they put a second class stamp on him and he arrived a week late, with his clothes torn and his right arm missing.

The groundsman was nailing up a sign over the school gates. He hit his thumb instead of the nail and broke the world record for throwing the hammer, and finding two hundred alternatives for the word 'bottom'.

The first event of the day was the three-legged race, which was won by Nureyev Major, by a good length.

Tempers were getting frayed in one corner of the field. . . Cowardly Major, our dormitory bully, had just thrown a vaulting-pole into the crowd — Bokowski, the Pole in question, won't be vaulting again for some time.

Having eaten twelve plates of sprouts and beans for his dinner, the ever-flatulent Methane Minor seemed to have that little something extra in the high jump, and cleared a record sixty-five feet over the cricket pavilion. . . Naturally, his beaten rivals said that he had benefited from a following-wind.

Then it was the main event of the day — The Marathon. Out came the starter. . . then came the soup. . . and the gun fired! Thirty-two fourth-formers slumped to the floor in slow motion — it was a machine gun. . . but the rest of us were off.

WEDNESDAY JUNE 25TH

Poor old Bunter Major, the disgusting fat pig of the Lower Remove, had yet another coronary after about a hundred and fifty yards, and he was severely thrashed for letting the school down, before being rushed off into Intensive Care.

While the Marathon was going on, Cowardly Major was busy laying landmines in the long-jump pit. . . and the parents were kept amused with other fringe events, like the sponsored flushing of Wimp Minor's head down the toilet. . . and Matron was running a 'Guess My Weight And You Can Have Me' stall alongside the potting sheds, with a sign saying, in small print, 'Twenty-five free guesses, and I'll give you ten stones lee-way either side. . .'

The Marathon was one of the fastest we'd ever run. I personally was back through the finishing-line before the second week in December. . .

But all this time, in the middle of the arena, they had been trying to get the inter-schools go-kart championships underway. Unfortunately, the Fishfriars go-kart engine just wouldn't start, but our top mechanic, Abdul Singh — a quiet boy with a perpetual aching head that he kept bandaged, presumably to help ease the pain — had the good sense to pinch another engine from a Japanese moped parked nearby. . . Yes. . . dear, oh-so-patient Diary — 'Ab's sense made the kart go Honda.'

As I lie here in my crawling-with-creatures cot, I muse on the oh so important question — Why is the fluff in your tummy button always grey, no matter what colour your clothes are. . .?

MONDAY JULY 7TH

It's almost the end of another school year at Fishfriars Hall. We've done our exams — every one was the same story — a bit like 'Quincey' really. After 20 minutes of each exam I found I had written all I could, and had filled almost half a side of the 20-page booklet we had been given. Then I looked around to see everybody else still writing away like mad.

Swotty Beaumont and every one of the girls had their hands up for extra sheets of paper. Sprinkler Peabody also had his hand up — all it takes is one question on crop irrigation or world rainfall and it's 'Man the pumps!' and 'Take to the lifeboats!' for anyone within a 100-yard radius of dear old Sprinkler.

Even Prince Luko, youngest member of The Royal Family, school halfwit, and next in line to somewhat curiously become President of The World Wildlife Preservation Society *and* Master of The Foxhunt, was still writing long after I'd finished. Bless him! He very nearly spelt his name *right* on one of the papers too!

The only area of inactivity was around Methane Minor — the chap voted least popular player in the school annual 'Sardines' championships — because his neighbours were clumped unconscious over their desks, due to the physical manifestations of our brussels sprout-eating classmate's exam nerves.

MONDAY JULY 7TH

There was a bit of a rumpus during our first exam when Dennis The Thorough Menace, Thatcher Major's hunk-of-a-man and school hip-flask-hiding champion, had to be carried out in a bucket. The Headmaster's official report said he was 'emotionally upset'. The News Of The World said 'He was emotionally upset as a newt.'

When the exams were over we all gathered outside — Swotty Beaumont bemoaning the fact that he'd only written forty-three sides before time was up — and everyone else saying what a mess they'd made of the paper. (The problem is I am always convinced that I am the only one who really means it.)

Exams over, Dr Frotter, our Headmaster, announced that we were all to take part in a mammoth War Game. This was an annual Fishfriars Hall event, designed to sort out the mice from the men. I squeaked loudly and scampered towards a hole in the skirting-board.

The Arch-Beako said that we were to be split into two for the game. Cowardly Major, our dormitory bully, obligingly started up his trusty chainsaw and had dissected half a dozen first formers before he was stopped and it was explained that was not quite what Dr Frotter had in mind.

Suddenly there was a loud inspiring cry — 'We'll fight on the beaches!' — Yes, it was Moron Maximus, the school skinhead. 'We'll fight in the amusement arcades. . . we'll fight in the bus station. . .'

The aim of the war-mongering Arch-Beako's blood-thirsty game was for one of the rival factions to capture the school buildings. Mr Hitler's eyes lit up at the thought. . . Wimp Minor's eyes also lit up, but that was because Cowardly Major had plugged him into the mains. . . Mr Hitler immediately went out and occupied the potting sheds — he also marched into the land designated for the site of the new latrine block — I suppose you could say, dear wailing-and-gnashing-of-teeth Diary, that he'd invaded 'Poe-land'.

Natural leaders emerged — Thatcher Major, as a female warrior, made Boadicea look a bit like the Avon Lady, and she bullied her way to becoming one leader, with Cowardly Major rapidly promoted to becoming her Personal Aide (it would have been Prince Luko, but we blew the Luko's Aide joke pages ago.) Mr Hitler already had half the chaps goose-stepping up and down the playground so we decided not to argue with fate. The two self-styled dictators took it in turn to choose their armies from the rest of the school. Soon there was only the chaff left that neither side wanted — Wimp Minor, Gender-Bender Major, Galtierri Maximus, and me. They had to draw short straws for us in the end. Collins Major, the extremely Senior Girl, was asked to form a Resistance Movement, but resistance proved not to be one of her strongest subjects.

When the ranks were all assembled, the Arch-Beako decided he wanted a record of this memorable occasion, so he commissioned the hiccoughing Dennis The Thorough Menace to paint the scene. Sadly Dennis incoherently declined — something about objecting to painting scenes which appertain to War — it seems he's just a 'Peace-Artist'. . .

The school chaplain came and spake unto our Army, his eyes glazing over with lust for glory, and yelled,

MONDAY JULY 7TH

'We are all Christians, and God will be with us in battle tomorrow, but nevertheless, if you don't get out there to gouge, maim, mutilate and kill, I'll have your bits and pieces on the Offertory Platter!!'

That night, contemplating the battle ahead, we sat round camp fires exchanging yarns. Gender-Bender Major was swopping a ball of grey yarn for a ball of pink yarn to knit himself his battle dress. . .

We were all lying outrageously about our previous conquests and the subject got on to the girls in the neighbouring WRAF Base. Tarbuck Major, the school big-head, suddenly burst into song, 'WAFs, I've had a few; But then again too few to mention. Boom-boom!' The self-contented chap laughed so much at his own joke that we had to stand him in a huge bowl to protect the tent.

Sitting round the campfire we all ate our supper of poached fish. MacFinaly Minor had just poached the fish from the nearby river — a lovely catch of fresh chub. Unfortunately, the bailiff had caught him and given him a bill for each of the poached chub. The Chaplain comforted the distressed young chap and said, 'Don't pay!' 'Trouble is, he saw my name on the name-tag on my kilt sir!' wailed the young Scot. To which the Chaplain suggested simply changing his name, and then with his bayonet, hacking into little pieces the bills for the chub and the name-tag from his kilt, and then he could be happy again. In actual fact, as he warmed his feet by the fire, he softly sang these unforgettable words, dear biting-on-a-bullet Diary — 'Hack up your chub bills and your old kilt-tag, and smile my child. . .'

MONDAY JULY 7TH

As I lie shivering in my billowing bivouac tonight, I think to myself — if Dennis The Thorough Menace, Thatcher Major's Company Mascot, is a self-made man — how come he didn't make himself a chin??

Matron and her special brand of 'tender loving care'

TUESDAY JULY 8TH

Dire Diary

Today was the day of the Battle of Fishfriars Hall, a mammoth War Game, whereby two teams aim to beat the opposition and capture the school buildings.

This promised to be a game of senseless bloodshed and violence to gain control of something that nobody really wanted in the first place. Thatcher Major had previous experience of this sort of thing, so she emerged as one leader. Mr Hitler, the other natural leader, had already seized Hells-Angel Minimus's swastika-daubed bicycle — or you could say, if you really must, dear can't-wait-till-it's-all-over Diary, he was holding a Nazi 'Raleigh'. . .

We camped out in the school playing-fields, awaiting the start of the battle at dawn. None of us slept much; I certainly didn't — I had to share a sleeping bag with Gender-Bender Major! The only ones who slept were a handful of unfortunates who were sharing a tent with Methane Minor. They had fallen into a deep coma, and our lusty Matron had to revive them with 'mouth-to-nose' resuscitation. One chap sneezed as he was coming round and increased her bust measurement by a good 4 inches! Our myopic Matron even got one asphyxiated little fellow upside down, but he didn't seem to mind. . .

At last it was dawn. The sun shyly peeped over the

neighbouring Nuclear Power Station, and the two-headed cockerel coughed all its feathers off.

Methane Minor sounded 'reveille' — he was Mr Hitler's 'Rear Bugler' — and not everyone can play bugle that way!

Our camp had already arisen. Thatcher Major had instructed her personal aide, Cowardly Major, to drill the younger boys before daybreak. Never one to miss an opportunity, he got his trusty Black & Decker and began perforating their skulls and kneecaps.

Suddenly the great oak doors of Fishfriars Hall flew open and out rode the Arch-Beako on his faithful charger, and the sparks began to fly — that is probably because, dear not-much-longer-to-go-now Diary, it was a battery charger. He had interrupted our makeshift breakfast of 'bully beef' — 'Bully beef' in this case being the legs of a cow that Cowardly Major had pulled off for something to do.

We had all been issued with eight dozen rounds of blanks. All except Bunter Major, the disgusting fat pig of the Lower Remove, who asked to be issued with eight dozen rounds of toasts instead, each thickly spread with condensed milk, strawberry jam and bloater paste.

Squinter Binns, the hairy-palmed dirty book collector and first reserve tent-pole for our encampment, went to the Armoury and traded 15 bundles of 'Wobbly Bits Weekly' for a couple of tanks. Tarbuck Major, the school big-head, leapt up dear about-to-rejoice-because-it's-all-over Diary, and sang 'Tanks for the mammaries. . .' The conceited chap laughed at his own joke so much he disappeared in a huge cloud of steam.

The local Archbishop, our guest of honour, fired a cannon to start the battle. The Canon in question was fired for gross misconduct, which had something to do with a choirboy, a pound and a half of rhubarb and a stirrup-pump.

The battle raged. Tactics varied. Thatcher Major introduced Light Infantry at the front. . . whereas Matron was introducing heavy adultery to a group of older boys at the rear.

Some chaps were selfishly hogging all the glory. Prince Luko, youngest member of the Royal Family, school half-wit and next in line to have a German magazine print a spurious report that he is actually the great grandson of Count Dracula and was responsible single-handed for The Great Train Robbery, The Crimean War, and the lousy weather in June — stepped forward to capture one of the opposition who had strayed towards us.

'Mine!' I yelled, 'Mine!'

'Nonsense little erk!' said the still-advancing Prince, 'He's not yours, I saw him first.' — and he was promptly blown up by a mine.

Suddenly Methane Minor dropped from the sky, greedily eating a huge bucketful of baked beans, mushy peas, sprouts, bran fibre and hard-boiled-eggs. 'Oh my God! said Thatcher Major, 'A surprise gas attack! Take cover!'

As we lay in our pungent trench, gasping for air, my thoughts were interrupted by another volley of gunshots and heavy mortar fire.

'Crickey you beasts!' shrieked Bunter Major,

'They're thowing shells at us now!'

'Ooh goody!' said Wimp Minor, 'If I hold one up to my ear, do you think I'll be able to hear the sea?' — He tried it and it blew his ear off!

We huddled in our cold, muddy trench and I took a drag on the Woodbine that was being passed round. 'God this is Hell!' said Attenborough Major, over-acting outrageously. 'It certainly is,' I choked, 'I don't smoke!'. . .

We were losing ground fast. Sprinkler Peabody, who was supposed to be guarding the school swimming-pool, sulked because Longford Maximus, the school spoil-sport had refused to lie down dead after being 'shot', so Sprinkler threw down his rifle and went off the deep end.

Suddenly there were some all-too-realistic screams, so we decided to surrender. After all it was only a game. 'We haven't got a white flag!' I said. . . 'I say! Use Wimp Minor's undies you chump!' trilled Bunter Major. 'You don't honestly believe they're still white do you?' sobbed the distraught little Wimp.

I ripped off my shirt, waved it above my head and emerged from the trench. Imagine my horror at the sight before me — bleeding bodies everywhere! A mysterious hooded figure with a machine-gun had some 'live' ammunition and was mowing everyone down. Dr Frotter had toppled from his charger; Methane Minor was rapidly deflating like a punctured barrage balloon; Matron was prostrated on her back — ever-hopeful, even in adversity; Mr Hitler was crawling, wounded, towards a coal-bunker, with a bottle of cyanide capsules; Prince Luko had been shot right through the head but fortunately was still walking about, whisting cheerfully. The hooded sniper was firing into our trench now — all my chums were collapsing in a bloody heap. Soon there only me left standing. The mystery gunman caught my eye — I suppose it was a pretty futile gesture throwing it at him in the first place. We stared at each other for a few moments — I tried to work out who he was. Was it the well-known drunk German gunman? I'm sure you know the one, dear bet-you-can-hardly-believe-we're-almost-there Diary — The pie-eyed sniper of Hammelin.

Cold-bloodedly he aimed and fired. As I felt the first bullet sear into my chest, I squealed. He told me not to squeal again or he would shoot off my tenth toe and injure me in such a way that my hair would drop out. In fact he actually sang the words. As I slumped to the floor, I heard him distantly singing this well-known battle-song, dear brace-yourself-this-is-definitely-the-last-one Diary — 'Squeal mate again; won't grow hair; no toe ten. . .'

As my consciousness slips away, I lie here thinking — will any of my chums survive?. . . Will Star Books want a sequel?. . . If Bombardier Methane Minor hadn't been shot, would he have gone on to do a remake of 'Winds of War'?. . . Who was the hooded figure with the live bullets?. . . Who hates Fishfriars Hall that much?. . . Come to think of it, who *doesn't* hate Fishfriars Hall that much?. . . Our publisher?. . . The controller of Capitol Radio?. . . Mary Whitehouse?. . . A reader who bought this book for their mum thinking it was a cookery book?. . . Will we ever know WHO SHOT FISHFRIARS HALL.

AUTHORS' FINAL NOTE

Mercifully that's it! We have posed lots of burning questions and hopefully before the sequel comes out we will have burnt the answers too.

Don't despair at the thought of a sequel, because when you bear in mind the pitiful state of the economy, rising unemployment, the escalation of nuclear weaponry, and the ever-present threat that 'Are You Being Served' might come back again, it doesn't seem quite as awful as you thought...not quite....

AUTHORS' OTHER FINAL NOTE

The authors wish it to be known that whilst it may be distressing to readers of a nervous disposition and other really weedy-wets, the violent ending to this diary is a serious and powerful climax befitting a book of this calibre - and is NOT in any way a purely commercial ploy to guarantee a sequel, or for tasteless and manipulative merchandising.

HURRY! HURRY!

Send now for your...

"WHO SHOT FISHFRIARS HALL?"...

... tee-shirts; sweat-shirts; night-shirts; vests; undies; mugs; tea-towels; lavatory paper; alarm clocks; corkscrews; novelty suppositories; baseball caps; money-boxes; little things which Boy Scouts use to get the stones out of horses' hooves; shoulder-bags; sweat-bands; bowls to be sick in after a particularly heavy night on the neighbour's home-brew; car-seat covers; pens; pencils; home-pregnancy-testing kits; notepaper; holdalls; nose-flutes; life-support machines; car stickers; badges; artificial insemination syringes; pencil-cases; carrier bags; crinkly-chip-making machines; tortoise-repellent cream; video games; ties; bomber-jackets; communications satellites; hand-guns; diaries; calendars; inflatable-rubber-woman-puncture outfits; seaside rock; Jumbo nose-picking sticks (please state length of trunk); key-rings; passport cases; nuclear war-heads; and many many more items...

ALSO – all the above are available with other choices of slogan...

* **"I SHOT FISHFRIARS HALL"**
* **"I WISH I'D SHOT FISHFRIARS HALL"**
* **"WHO CARES WHO SHOT FISHFRIARS HALL?"**
* **"I WISH SOMEONE WOULD SHOOT ALL THE STUPID PRATTS WHO WALK ABOUT WITH 'WHO SHOT FISHFRIARS HALL?' ON THEIR SHIRTS"**
* **"I AM A TOTALLY GULLIBLE NINNY WHO BUYS EVERY BIT OF OVER-PRICED TATTY MERCHANDISING CRAP THE PROFITEERING SHARKS HAVE TO OFFER"**

PRICES ON APPLICATION (Please state how gullible you are)

If you order THREE or more of the above items, we will realise we've got a right 'nana', and will send you *FREE* a list of other ridiculous items that you can buy at even more exorbitant prices.

ALSO... **Why not send a petition to your local M.P. and get him to lobby Star Books to publish a sequel to reveal "Who shot Fishfriars Hall?"... (and don't forget to insist that the authors get paid more next time.)**